- Dozens of books have been written, explaining the changes in this country over the past fifteen years.

- All of them assume that there is a single "young" viewpoint; all of them equate change with progress and morality with convenience.

- It is time somebody spoke up for millions of young people who think differently: who believe in excellence, in morality, in values; who are not prepared to accept the destruction of government, schools, churches, and family life — institutions which are the very life-blood of a healthy nation.

- A young man *has* spoken up. He has written this book for you who share his ideals.

THE
MORALITY GAP

THE
MORALITY GAP

Mark Evans

ALBA BOOKS
DIV. OF SOC. OF ST. PAUL · CANFIELD, OHIO 44406

Library of Congress Card Number: 76-6702

ISBN 0-8189-1132-8

© Copyright 1976 by Alba House Communications,
  Canfield, Ohio 44406

Printed in the United States of America

TO MY PARENTS

THE
AUTHOR

MARK EVANS is a young Californian of many interests and the talents to pursue them successfully.

He is a prolific and versatile writer. Among his previous books are SOUNDTRACK: THE MUSIC OF THE MOVIES; THE SPECTACULAR STUNT BOOK (devoted to the amazing exploits of movie stuntmen) and SCOTT JOPLIN AND THE RAGTIME YEARS.

He is host of *"Mark My Words!"* a syndicated radio program.

As a composer, conductor and lyricist, his latest musical is "Going Around in Academic Circles," a satire on college life based on the writings of Richard Armour.

He is greatly in demand as a speaker and holds M.A. and Ph.D degrees from Claremont Graduate School.

TABLE OF CONTENTS

INTRODUCTION

In a time of angry outrage, I sat down at the typewriter to write the book you are about to read. It was originally published under the title, *"Will the Real Young America Please Stand Up?"*, and its purpose, then, as now, was to commit to paper my reactions to the youth culture.

More specifically, I wanted to shatter for all time a myth which seemed to be gaining widespread popularity, that the fads and fashions, the morals and mystiques of the counter-culture represented an advance in civilization.

Since the publication of this book in hardcover, the country as a whole and our individual communities have survived a number of traumatic events. The Vietnam War, regarded by many as the most divisive issue in modern times ended. The Watergate episode occupied our national attention with the curious fascination unique to a scandal. More directly related to this book, the image of the counterculture's chief advocate, the hippie-dropout changed. Many of the dropouts of the late 1960's have dropped back into the mainstream of society, bringing with them a dubious legacy. The issues and causes they initiated, the ones I have criticized in these pages, have not disappeared; they have merely taken new guises.

As the 1970's move to a close, we may well ask ourselves where the flower children (or their ideological mentors) have gone? We need not look far. The rock groups may have moved from the outdoor arena to the concert hall, with full blessings of the local symphony association. Those who proselytize the drug culture may be found distributing leaflets urging that their habits be legalized. The campus radical has very probably joined the faculty, and goes to class to expound his views three days a week. As for the champions of that unfashionable phenomenon I have dubbed "slobbism", they have quietly become pacesetters for the new fashion: as movie stars or just members of the family.

The basic questions of the self-proclaimed new morality or the overall attack on our past culture as irrelevant continue. The call to arms of the underground press has been joined (and echoed) by a variety of psychologists and sociologists. In short, the counterculture has tried to achieve by assimilation what it could not accomplish through cultural revolution: respectability.

If the wild-eyed militant of several years ago seems to have mellowed, perhaps it is in part because our society has started to accept some of his attitudes. Whether or not this is constructive is one of the great issues facing each and every one of us in our daily lives. It is my belief, and one I believe to be shared by many others, that the dropout counterculture was basically "Counter" and had very little to do with culture. If the youth cult of this period was a dismal failure with its principal advocates outside our social mainstream, we stand to accomplish nothing by borrowing their empty notions now that they have dropped back in.

In truth, many of our institutions, especially the family, are threatened more by the present advocates of non-culture: the academicians, psychologists, and sociologists, who have the technical jargon to verbalize concepts which the inarticulate rebels could only advocate through a lifestyle. A pontificating theoretician may do more to undermine the basis of morality or common sense than a thousand violent revolutionaries. But failure to recognize their common bond is folly. The professor or writer who assures us that the family, the home, the church, the government, and our collected books, music, and art, are outdated institutions, differs little from the dropout. They both seek to reject the same things.

When the hardcover edition of this book appeared in print, I naturally expected controversy. There was a specific reaction, however, which did surprise me. It was widespread and voiced often enough to be indicative of a basic attitude which exists in our society. A large number of persons, especially in the book trade and media, assumed, often without reading the book in advance, or questioning its author, that they understood the origin and purpose of my objections to the counterculture. There is a popular view among some self-styled intellectuals that these opinions can only be attributed to a lack of sophistication. They further assume, without question, that political paranoia is offensive only to the naive, but well-meaning citizen; that the multi-billion dollar rock phenomenon repels only those whose musical tastes are in the gay 90's; that drugs or slobbism or moral erosion are objectionable only in the minds of cloistered librarians, latter-day Carrie Nations, and men with the declining vigor of Elmer Fudd. In short, they have decided that the counterculture can easily define its critics; little old ladies in tennis shoes, right-wing reactionaries seeking to turn back the clock, and provincial misanthropes with an ignorant antipathy toward progress in general and the latest ideology from the big city in particular.

All of this is blatant nonsense, and should be recognized as such.

It is high time that we recognize the facts of life. The movement discussed in this book is unique in our history because it challenges the foundations of our culture. The cacophonous frauds of the rock record industry have, creatively and commercially, chosen to exclude and absorb any and all media of musical expression. The cause of this book is not that of the unsophisticated listener who boasts of a tin ear and a yearning for the good old days. Rather, it is those who realize that it is time for all those who love good music, from the classics to jazz, to speak out in the name of literacy. A hit record, by any other name, can still be a fraud. The deafening amplified guitars have drowned out the symphony composer and the jazz combo. The "like'y'know, where it's at, what's happening" writers have silenced the pens of writers who still regard the English language as a passionate and eloquent art form, rich and vibrant in its capacity for expression.

The ideological critics have decided that man's humanity is irrelevant to artistic growth. Instead of encouraging us to aspire to high ideals, they present us with undisciplined arrogance, glorying in their commonness.

It should be unnecessary to indulge in disclaimers, but for any who are interested, right-wing reactionaries have proven themselves as ridiculous as left-wing radicals long ago, and tennis shoes should be worn when it's time for tennis. As for the intelligentsia, trying to quote Thoreau from his jail cell, asking "What are you doing out there? ", I pose the following query: "What are *you* doing on the side of the non-culture? "

There is also an assumption that advocates of our traditional concept of morals are tight-lipped Puritans ready to promise hellfire and damnation to all who stray from the most minor suggestion of Emily Post. Tolerance may be one of man's nobler qualities, but it is no reason to dash out and join the nearest orgy.

In short, the voices of reason, logic, and common sense, have been silent for too long. For fear of seeming foolish, many of us have been ready to leave civilized society to the barbarians. It is those of us who cherish a meaningful culture who have the responsibility of defending it against the onslaught. The ignorant cannot defend what they do not know or understand; the pseudo-sophisticate is too busy thinking of his place in history, so history passes him by.

Benjamin Franklin's old adage about either hanging together or hanging separately is as valid today as when our country was founded. The survival of our values can only be achieved collectively, by rugged individualists with the courage of their convictions. A voice in the wilderness has now been sounded; whether or not you hear it, and what you choose to answer, is up to you.

PREFACE

As an author who prefers to express himself through ideas rather than through a first-person narrative, I shall include no personal references in the forthcoming pages. However, I believe it necessary to explain briefly my reasons for devoting considerable time and space to a discussion of the young men and women of my generation.

During the past decade, America has been obsessed with youth. No aspect of daily living has been free from influence by a set of customs, mannerisms, sounds, attitudes, and prejudices which are generally identified will all young Americans. Some persons refer to this movement as the "counterculture"; I choose to call it the "youth cult."

Although millions of Americans have been demonstrably hostile to this cult, large numbers of highly vocal citizens have taken the opposite view. They purport to "understand" the trials and tribulations of young America. They advertise their receptive attitudes toward "young ideas" and dismiss dissenters as antiquated specimens, too ignorant or unsophisticated to progress with the times.

The philosophy and literature of the youth cult have been confused and erratic. Books explaining the changes that have affected America during the last fifteen years range from the primitive obscenities of the campus radicals to sophisticated academic studies. Sociologists and psychologists approach these problems with a scholarly, clinical attitude, while commercial writers strive to inform the public in the most schocking ways possible of the latest traditions which are to be discarded in the name of progress.

All of these books (and their widely publicized authors) have one quality in common: they assume without question that there is a single "young" viewpoint to which sophisticated young adults generally subscribe. They equate change with progress and morality with convenience; they are permeated by inaccuracies and superficial, simplistic conclusions. Most of all, they literally deny the existence of those members of the youngest generation who do not support their theories.

By way of introduction I must add a personal note. I do not have to prove my youth or rationalize my own capacity for achievement. I have no axe to grind, no ideological mission, no personal vendetta to conclude. But apologists for the youth cult do not speak for me. They do not speak for the thousands of young men and women who, like me, have survived academic inequities, bureaucratic stupidity, and often brutal assaults upon our ideals because we believed that the world be made a better place through individual accomplishement and mature responsibility.

The most thoughtful and passionate of our youth believe in excellence, in morality, and in values. The youth cult is diametrically opposed to all of these elements. We have been compelled to witness the birth of a perverse and warped culture, presumably representing our generation, aided and abetted by an absurd group of middle-aged adults frightened beyond belief at the prospect of growing old.

At the heart of the youth cult is distorted, twisted standard. Honors, adulation, and the mantle of respectability are reserved for those who achieve the ultimate in mediocrity, immorality, and hyprocrisy. Those of us who believe in the viability of traditional values are described as "irrelevant" to our own generation.

History has proven that men and ideas may both be measured by what they stand for, rather than what they stand against. Those who see the events of the 1960's and 1970's, as a great step forward do us a disservice. They make it difficult, if not impossible, for constructive, positive revitalization of those customs and institutions that are the bulwark of freedom and a civilized society.

We are not satisfied with the world. We are not complacent in the face of war, poverty, disease, or decay. We want the same things our parents wanted, the same goals to which man has eternally aspired. Unfortunately, we stand between two extremes in society. One extreme desires the status quo; the other seeks to enact change for the sake of change, change at any price. After all the philosophical analysis, sociological speculation, academic jargon, metaphysical expostulation, and epistemological theory has ended, what does the youth cult offer us? A society in which the singularly important components are drug addiction, indiscriminate sex, dirt, filth, ignorance, illiteracy, and cultural Yahooism; in short, verbal niceties are employed to defend slobbism.

We believe that the greatest threat facing our country today is the segment of middle-aged adults who seek to turn over our culture and our society to those members of our generation who are least qualified to sustain it and most likely to destroy it. A responsible youth today has few places to go. He is not welcome in the groves of academe, where radicals are greeted and reformers are ignored. He is not welcome in the creative arts, where standards of taste have become so commercialized that a lack of talent is often considered a prime advantage in the prognosis for success. He may be considered eligible for the business world, but only if he subscribes to predetermined concepts of "youthfulness" in his manners, dress, and speech.

We are told constantly that America's hope is in its youth. This may well be the case, but only if we do not vulgarize the term "youth" to encompass anyone who happens to have lived for a prescribed number of years. America's real leaders have tried to devote themselves to learning, to preparation, to study, and most important, to self-development. America's hope is its forgotten young Americans who do not subscribe to the youth cult.

Our generation needs leaders, not political schemers; demands accomplishment, not the debunking of excellence. It requires values of substance, not moral erosion. It is ironic that apologists for the youth cult, so ready and eager to "understand," to "communicate," to "listen," and not incidentally to "imitate" and to "conform," have made our world all the harder. In their world, the unwashed ignoramus becomes the hope for the future; the responsible young man or woman becomes a curiosity, an oddity; and a vestigial manifestation of a society in its decline.

When academicians try to portray us as custodians of the status quo, they insult our intelligence, mock our values, ridicule our imagination, and do all of these things in the name of "understanding youth." Young Americans everywhere may worry about their futures, their families, their work at school or in their careers. They are often compelled to ask: "Is there a place for me? " When they see ostensibly mature adults ready to turn society upside-down to cater to a select element of youth which proclaims itself the hope of America, they are compelled to believe that the answer is "No."

Some young Americans are tired of being dismissed as irrelevant, conservative, old-fashioned, and out-of-date. Some middle-aged Americans are tired of being subjected to ridicule and abuse because they approach their children as leaders, not followers. Both these groups of Americans are tired of hippies, Yippies, and malcontents. They are tired of a sub-culture that cannot survive without depending on drugs or stimulants. They are tired of rock musicians, poets, artists and writers who are so totally lacking in even a single shred of ability that they compelled Ernest Hemingway to call this "The Millennium of the Untalented." They are tired of seeing dirty, filthy, unwashed slobs being glorified as heroes. They are tired of a culture whose vocabulary demands vulgarity, coarseness, and obscenity. They are no longer able to tolerate the demise of taste or the apotheosis of slobbism. Most of all, they will refuse to countenance the efforts of those poor, misguided adults who should know better to offer this new culture as the only alternative for America.

They will totally reject efforts to proclaim a new society which is established by tearing down the government, the schools, the churches, the families, and the institutions which are the very life-blood of a healthy nation. They seek a return to morals, values, and a meaningful culture in the most sophisticated sense. They realize that an X-rated film, an underground newspaper, and a uniform of dirty clothing does not make a philosopher or a moral sage any more that the ability to wave the flag makes one a patriot. They will turn back the philosophical assault on the home, the family, and a real sense of values. They recognize the exciting, dynamic, positive alternatives that do exist today. They seek a return to common sense in America. They know the youth cult is not the only alternative because they are the real alternative.

I have written this book for them.

I.

THE MORALITY GAP:
CASTING IN STEREOTYPE

What we call Progress is the exchange of one nuisance for another nuisance .... Havelock Ellis

Zeal without knowledge is like fire without a grate to contain it; like a sword without a hilt to wield it by; like a high-bred horse without a bridle to guide him. It speaks without thinking, acts without planning, seeks to accomplish a good end without the adoption of becoming means .... Julius Bate

If any subject may be said to arouse an emotional response in the hearts and minds of men it is today's youth. Americans may be found who subscribe to every possible faith, creed, or personal philosophy. But it is difficult to find any American who has not addressed himself at one time or another in the recent past to the question of our young people: where they have been, where they are, and most important of all, where they are going. Mention the youth of America in your local barbershop, grocery store, or police station. Remind a successful corporate executive or a labor-union leader about his children. Question your clergyman or high-school principal about the activities of the younger generation. The spectrum of responses will be infinite and contradictory. Undoubtedly, at least one person will suggest that young Americans are tools of the devil, bent upon their

own destruction (and everyone else's), eager to earn a place
for themselves in the raging fires of hell. Another popular
response is that the young, referred to vaguely as "the kids,"
are not to blame for our current political and social difficulties, and that if the mature-adult community will only
abandon its hostile or lethargic state, the young will lead it
out of the wilderness.

Obviously, such emotional responses do little in the way
of explaining why many young people behave as they do;
true understanding requires penetrating, in-depth analysis.
Occasionally, someone tries to interpret America's growing
youth culture, proposing to explain the whys and wherefores
of young Americans, with emphasis on discerning a logical
pattern of events that may render a new, subtle coherence to
occurrences that have seemed otherwise incomprehensible.

The decade of the 1960's was a time of radical change for
America. At one time, politicians used to suggest that the
flag, motherhood, and apple pie were subjects which could
never be publicly criticized. But during the 1960's, every
imaginable taboo in our daily lives was challenged, if not
altered. Because these changes occurred on a gradual basis,
some social observers were not quick to recognize that the
combination of all these elements together could result in a
new political, social, and cultural revolution. Many of the
ways in which society has changed are so well-known as to
make their retelling unnecessary. Ultimately, the culture,
dress, attitudes, music, and drugs with which many young
persons identified became known as the "counterculture."
The counterculture has its own literature, its own music and
films, its own political activities, and its own heroes. Today,
many Americans have forgotten about the counterculture.
The Vietnam War has moved from the military to the political spectrum; the college campuses have quieted down; the
1970's seem, superficially, more stable, more calm, and we
seem headed back toward normalcy.

The illusion is desirable but unjustified. In the 1970's,
many of the influences of the counterculture are still alive.
But they have moved directly into the mainstream of society. One reason for the change is that many influences of

the 1960's youth revolution have been welcomed, promoted, and defended by a large, articulate, and highly influential group of citizens. These men and women often describe themselves as liberal and open-minded; they say that they believe that this new revolution, the expression of the new youth culture, will be a peaceful non-violent cultural upheaval which will change our lives and our values simultaneously and for the better.

These men and women are active in the educational world, in publishing, and in the news media; they all affect our communications, the means whereby Americans learn what other Americans are thinking. For the most part, they have portrayed our social ills in terms of a generation gap. In a gross oversimplification, they have chosen to identify a number of social and political attitudes with young people; in a neat and curious dichotomy, they divide the rest of society into two groups: those who understand the kids and those who don't.

The result of this occurrence is that many Americans have come to accept stereotypes and pre-fashioned images and definitions. The generation gap has been portrayed as a struggle between our "young people" and their middle-aged supporters, who want to change the whole direction of our society, and the old-fashioned, antiquated men and women who are too unsophisticated or narrow-minded to appreciate these changes.

Because of this emphasis on the generation gap, many Americans have proceeded to draw conclusions about the younger generation. Ideas are labeled "young" or "old." Much of our society remains unaware that many young Americans do not subscribe to the ideas which are set forth as representing the younger generation. The existence of a large segment of America's young people has been ignored by professors, writers, publishers, sociologists, and the news media. Why has this happened?

The error lies in the failure to recognize that the generation gap is not really a struggle between the young and the old, but rather between two value systems. For obvious reasons, one value system has chosen to wrap itself in the

mantle of progress, change, and youthful idealism. It is difficult to oppose ideas which are advanced under this banner;
it is socially unfashionable and one runs the risk of being
called a variety of names, all of which are most unpleasant.
It is easier to praise the new youth revolution as a splendid
example of twentieth-century progress.

Many Americans do not realize that the idea of the generation gap is a direct result of an unconscious conspiracy
between some well-meaning but thoroughly misguided individuals. Whenever the subject of conspiracy is raised, the
person who calls attention to the subject is ridiculed. Admittedly, there are those who think that there are Communists
hiding under every bed, and their efforts to wake up America seem more laughable or pathetic than serious. But this
conspiracy, as previously stated, has been unconscious. It is a
difficult and bizarre occurrence to describe.

For the last several decades, a large segment of the professors, liberal by their own definition, have expounded their
political and social views. Some of these men are distinguished scholars in a specific field; some do not have the
common sense to come in out of the rain. Their academic
credentials may be impressive and tend to blur this fact. The
professors have taught young men and women who have
gone on to become journalists, reporters, sociologists, writers, and politicians; many have participated in various aspects of the news media. These individuals in the communications field spend their time commenting on American
society, and making their ideas known to the public. The
effect tends to be cyclical: the professors teach their students who later write books. The books are reviewed by
critics who are favorable to the views of the professors. The
news media men read the books, with their favorable critical
reviews, and report on the events they see taking place in
the nation. Being human, they often allow their personal
views to color their reports. The professors listen to the
news reports, which have been written by journalists, some
of whom appear to investigate on a subjective level, finding
those new stories that reinforce their views.

The cycle starts all over again when the professors react to the news stories by reinforcing their views. These men and women talk to each other, read the same books, share the same ideas. They pride themselves on being intellectual. They are often extremely articulate to the point of glibness. This tends to confuse those who do not share their verbal facility but who feel uncomfortable with their arguments. In turn, these men and women go around in an intellectual circle. They thrive on pseudo-intellectual snobbery, because they all read the "best books," belong to the "best political groups," study the attitudes of the "most brilliant thinkers." Many of these men and women live and work in the East, provoking some bitter resentment against an Eastern clique. They often seem oblivious to the prevailing views of Americans in the Midwest and South. But it would be a great mistake to portray this problem in geographic terms. Every section of the country has its share of ignoramuses, well-educated or otherwise.

In the 1960's, these men and women exercised a profound influence on our society by persuading us of the nature of the youth-cult revolution. They failed to recognize the true nature of the "generation gap"; in fact, books, ideas, and activities that did not reinforce their preconceived views were ignored or ridiculed. Now in the 1970's, these same men and women are advising us to "learn from our mistakes of the 1960's." They have learned little themselves.

Before writing this book, I was advised by experts on the publishing field that the critics and reviewers are all on the other side; the book will never have a chance, even though it tells the truth. The pseudo-intellectual and critical élite of this country do not want to be forced to look at the reality of the counterculture or its more respectable assimilation into mainstream society.

There are many in the United States today who pride themselves on their objectivity, but they thrust their heads into the ground when confronted with the fact that many young people do not subscribe to the youth cult or its promoters in any age bracket.

6 THE MORALITY GAP

In this book, the reader is invited to join the author in exploring the counterculture of the 1960's and to examine its influence on the 1970's. We shall quickly learn that the revolution of our young people is not representative of our young people at all, but of a segment of all generations. It is a bizarre story in which America's values are turned upside-down. In many ways, this nation's upheavals have resembled Alice's Wonderland. Most of the central figures in this story wear bizarre clothing and behave in strange ways. Some are irreverent, and like the Cheshire Cat, are grinning and smirking for no reason at all. Some, like the Duchess who continues sneezing while pouring pepper into a baby's soup, continue to ferment trouble and agitate for changes; they do not realize that these changes are misguided and often evil. There are many academicians, who seem to have borrowed Lewis Carroll's "curriculum" of Reeling, Writing, and all the parts of Arithmetic: ambition, distraction, uglification, and derision. There is a villain, of course, vaguely defined as the Establishment, and a chorus of shrill voices screaming, "Off with their heads."

America, in short, has been conducting a Mad Tea Party. The invited guests have been too bewildered to understand what has happened. Like Alice, they are still trying to find their way home.

Let us examine some commonly used labels. We shall quickly see how terms are often confused, and how we can persuade ourselves that up is down and right is wrong.

The hosts of our Mad Tea Party have assumed that Americans can be divided into neat categories. Some citizens, we are told, are "conservative." They want to return to an imaginary yesterday in which America was a nation of small towns and simple virtues. They select their political candidates on the basis of morality; they yearn for the past days of reliance on private business, abolition of welfare, and reawakening of vigilance against domestic subversion. In contrast to the backward conservatives, we are able to find the "liberals." By their own definition, the liberals are better educated, more sophisticated, more open-minded than conservatives.

The classic commercial images of conservatives and liberals are the television characters, Archie Bunker and Maude Findlay. Both characters were developed through the production endeavors of Norman Lear. Both characters have become part of American folklore through the success of "All in the Family" and "Maude" on television. Archie Bunker is a funny, ridiculous caricature, skillfully portrayed by Carroll O'Connor. But Archie is unappealing, ignorant, and bigoted. We may laugh at "All in the Family," but we don't want to be like Archie. Even the real Archies laugh at the Bunkers because they don't see themselves reflected in Archie's image. "Maude" was initially announced as a satire of the die-hard liberal. Allegedly, the show would portray the other side of the coin. C. H. Simonds, in a column entitled "The Honesty Trap" sees through the façade with this observation. "Loudmouthed, featherheaded, flatulent, enuretic though she may be, Maude is by-golly on the side of the angels, she's right to have the abortion, Peace Now. Counterbalance to Archie Bunker, my foot. Come Message Time, Archie and all he stands for (bigotry, narrowness, insensitivity; also patriotism, hard work, traditional morality) are usually shot down in flames."

These last elements, patriotism, hard work, and traditional morality, are publicly identified with ignorant, ill-educated bigotry (Archie) or stupidity (his wife Edith). In turn, "Maude" continues to perpetuate these images by pretending to satirize the liberals and social reformers while trumpeting their ideological causes.

Not everyone who believes in hard work or traditional morality is an ill-educated bigot with little ability to perceive the great philosophical or moral issues of our time. The fact that intelligent, highly liberate conservatives find themselves on the same side as Archie Bunker on some issues does not mean that they are unsophisticated ignoramuses, any more that the critical élite's meek, misty-eyed tolerance of Marxism or anarchy means that members of the press corps are personally Communists or anarchists.

Advocates of the youth cult like Archie as a foil. He's a wonderful target, because many Americans will check their

common sense at the door to make themselves feel progressive (unlike Archie!). The image of a plodding, ignorant,
corrupt, bigoted Establishment is a convenience for the hosts
of our Mad Tea Party. They offer a steady diet of the youth
cult, with the veiled threat that unless we want to be as
stupid as the Bunkers, we'd better sit down and have some
tea.

Let us examine some typical redefinitions. Progress, we
are told, is redefined as change. If we accept this neat notion, we assume that any idea is valid because it is new. But
change is not synonymous with progress. A tornado may
"change" a town by levelling it; this does not imply constructive alteration by any means.

Russel Kirk has expressed the idea eloquently: "Recognition that change and reform are not identical, and that
innovation is a devouring conflagration more often than it is
a torch of progress. Society must alter, for slow change is a
means of conservation, like the human body's perpetual
renewal; but Providence is the proper instrument for change,
and the test of a statesman is his cognizance of the real tendency of Providential social forces."

The plight of the working man is eloquently retold, with
one small alteration. The worker's struggle is based upon
conditions which existed at the time of Samuel Gompers. We
cannot evaluate the relationship between modern corporations and the AFL – CIO as governed by George Meany's
administration in the same terms. But since it suits the political motives of the New Left to treat labor relations in
these terms, the advocates of the New Politics are not to be
restrained.

Once we become accustomed to these redefinitions, we
can easily recognize how arguments can become distorted.
For example, the television and news media devote considerable attention to the women's liberation movement. More
often than not, their viewpoint is presented as the "woman's
view." No qualifications are needed. The critical élite who
read the best books and communicate with the most brilliant
intellectuals realize that there is only one woman's view. The
other women are Edith Bunkers.

Mrs. Helen B. Andelin, a Santa Barbara mother of eight, wrote a book called *Fascinating Womanhood*. Major publishers rejected the book because obviously it was unrelated to the cultural mainstream as seen by the women's liberationists. Mrs. Andelin proposed that, "A woman can gain true happiness in marriage by placing the husband's happiness as a primary goal." Mrs. Andelin's book, which counseled women to cultivate feminity and stay away from the business world, sold over 200,000 copies. But Mrs. Andelin had to publish her book through her own company because the publishers were being "open-minded" about the woman's view, the only one they recognize.

When 150 members of the American Society for Divorced Men picketed the Civic Center Plaza in Chicago, the *New York Times* was disinterested. The newspaper gave the men a small paragraph in the back of the paper; only men favoring women's liberation could get front-page coverage.

This attitude toward women is similar to the view of young people. Only those young people whose views approximate those of the critical élite are recognized with any validity.

Consider some specific examples of controversies relating to the generation gap. Imagine that you encountered these issues without any preconceived knowledge of the redefinition game that is played by our social advisors.

A high-school newspaper is published by some students who are registered at the high school. The newspaper is not the official school publication, but is distributed on campus by these students on their own. The principal or the school board objects to the newspapers, and plans are made to ban them from the campus. An outcry is raised; the school administration is foolish and unimaginative. They have bowed to pressure from a parent who vaguely resembles Archie Bunker. The American Civil Liberties Union steps into the battle. We hear demands for free speech and quotations from Thomas Jefferson.

Superficially, the image we receive is typical of the generation gap: our "young people" being stifled by old-fash-

ioned adults who are too backward to appreciate their
creativity or their free spirits.

Now before you join the bandwagon and begin shouting
about what the Establishment is doing to "our children,"
examine the following description of the high-school underground newspaper that caused the controversy.

This newspaper contained every variety of four-letter
word; it abounded in obscenities. One similar newspaper
devoted considerable attention to student demonstrations.
Special attention was devoted to relationships with the police, including such topics as "How to behave when a cop
frisks you." Advice of this kind is common: "Local cops and
the FBI may question you. Don't answer! You have a right
to remain silent." The article concludes with references to
students who should prepare to wear helmets, and expect
tear gas or mace. Exercising their free speech, the students
go on to declare, "Don't bring your address book; if you are
busted, the cops will get the names of all your friends."

One "student newspaper" issues its demands: open admission to colleges, no suspensions or expulsions, freedom of
speech, freedom of the press, establishment of Black, Puerto
Rican, and Radical Studies courses, end to the tracking
systems, cops, narcs, and security guards out of the schools!
"We're making a revolution – join us! "

Police officers are referred to as "pigs." Demands are
issued which essentially call for the administration to surrender its authority to control the students' activities. Presumably, these students want to choose their own courses,
inevitably of the Marxist or anarchist variety, violate the
drug laws on campus with sanction of the school authorities,
and devote their class time to promoting a political revolution for the New Left. They also want permission to distrib-
ute these materials, urging other students to join in the fun.

On what basis are high school students, fortunate to have
made average grades in a beginning United States history
course, entitled to rewrite the curriculum, run the school,
violate the laws, preach their obscenities and revolutionary
schemes, *to the exclusion* of all other students who do not
subscribe to their beliefs?

Yet efforts to limit this type of activity are predictable; the "progressives" talk about freedom of the press, and the poor student radicals who are being denied the "right," at the ripe old age of fifteen or sixteen to turn the high-school campus into a revolutionary cell.

The second example is the police department that announces a plan to search student's lockers without their permission. Immediately, we are reminded of a police state without the protection against search and seizure. The media, the interpreters, the open-minded progressives, join "the kids" in their idealistic protest against the grim, intimidating police villians.

Before you join the hue and cry about police brutality, consider the following:

A man signs in as a visitor to an elementary school during "Open School Week," then enters a classroom and robs the teacher.

A group of non-students enter a high-school campus and assault a school administrator.

Gang members are seen carrying sawed-off shotguns on campus.

A suspect is stopped by police on the steps of the high school; he is carrying an eight-inch kitchen knife.

A high-school student is arrested for carrying a .38 caliber revolver.

Five girls, including two high-school students, stripped and beat a fifteen-year-old girl from another high-school.

A teenage boy shoves a ninety-year-old woman to the sidewalk during a purse snatching; she dies, he gets a dollar.

Sixty gun episodes take place in Los Angeles in a single school year.

Fifteen handguns are confiscated in Atlanta schools. A twelve-year-old boy, who disobeyed traffic signals, was angry at other students who laughed at him. He opened fire on the school ground.

Fifteen gun incidents occur in each of the following cities in a single year: Detroit, New York, Kansas City.

The decision by the police to search the students' lockers is denounced by advocates of student rights; these civil libertarians are evidently not disturbed regarding another student right. This right belongs principally to those non-militants who do not issue non-negotiable demands: the right to attend school and go to class without being shot.

Arthur Miller, a distinguished playwright, published a statement asking if we can doubt that all of our problems — war, poverty, discrimination, and every other misfortune — would disappear from the earth if everyone over thirty simply vanished. He also makes a plea for misguided adults to stop "turning against our children."

Often advocates of the youth cult are articulate, famous, and accomplished in the scholarly or artistic fields. Miller's assumption is that of "youthful innocence" and "mature corruption." He assumes that a society composed exclusively of the young would be idealistic, pure, and totally founded on moral principles. Miller forgets that the young, like everyone else, are people; the younger generation has its members who achieve the extremes of good and evil; most are somewhere in between.

Consider the following examples of "our children" at work and play:

The *New York Times* reports an increase of 174% in shoplifting. More than fifty percent are juveniles, especially suburban junior-high-school youngsters.

A school girl arrested for shoplifting describes her motive: "To prove I was groovy."

Another juvenile shoplifter describes a club in which the admission requirement is stealing, combined with successful lying to one's parents about the real source of the stolen goods.

Five hundred high-school students walk out of class, set fire to a basement, then run around the neighborhood, in the words of the student paper, "doing things."

A fire starts early in the morning, and a high-school is evacuated. Four hundred students, visit the principal to present their "non-negotiable" demands.

High-school students burn an American flag and go on a rampage throughout the school.

Arthur Miller should remember that Willy Loman, in *Death of a Salesman*, was destroyed partially by his lack of perception regarding himself and the world around him. Not all high-school students engage in the above activities. But these are the students who receive sympathetic attention in the press.

In recent months it has become fashionable to tag labels on to citizens. Of prime importance is one's classification. In the past, being an American meant just that. The man who emphasized age, sex, race in making decisions was practicing discrimination. Now, however, labeling has become important. Like Arthur Miller, a large segment of the population assumes the sanctity and purity of ideas which ostensibly emanate from the younger generation. These well-meaning citizens are so busy being receptive to the young that they never stop to ask themselves what happens to the students who do *not* side with the militants, the young men and women who do not share the attitudes of the counterculture?

In the business world, youth has become a prime selling point. The maxim, never trust anyone over thirty, has been transformed, Madison Avenue style, into "Never hire anyone over thirty." The emphasis on youth has forced a continued cycle of dependence on the noisiest, most radical, least responsible segment of our youthful population. On close examination, the social analysts are trying to divide society into categories right out of a Hollywood B-Western. Those who do not favor an integration in society of those attitudes and behavioral practices of the youth cult are portrayed as villains, in favor of wars, repression, pollution, and perhaps even the common cold. The heroes are supposed to be young, creative, dynamic, and progressive.

In the coming pages, we shall examine some basic attitudes and elements of the counterculture of the 1960's, with their new relevance to controversies of the 1970's; we shall consider the culture of some young people which is offered mistakenly in the name of young people. We shall see why many Americans find this new culture abhorrent, why it can be rejected by both young and old, and why its open-

minded advocates have closed minds when dealing with this
brand of criticism. Some of these elements will be theore-
tical, dealing with the whys and wherefores of radical politics; others will be cultural, concerned with music, films,
literature, and fashions; still others will deal with medical
questions (i.e., drugs) and morality.

Ultimately, we will recognize this new youth cult as an
assault upon our traditional values. The youth cult cannot
succeed without the abolition or radical alteration of most
of our traditional institutions and attitudes toward the
family, marriage, the work ethic, traditional artistic standards,
taste, manners, republican form of government, and morality. The facts will speak for themselves. An examination
of the youth cult will quickly reveal it to be hollow, hypocritical and superficial. Instead, we will consider the alternatives.

In exploring the world of the youth culture, we shall
make some startling discoveries. First, it will become increasingly clear that today's crisis is not a conflict between the
old and the new, between parental and younger generations.
It is rather between those of all generations who believe in a
traditional concept of ethics and morality, and those who do
not. There are those who believe in a fixed basis for morality, those who see right and wrong as constants, not varia-
bles. There are also those who believe that right and wrong
are movable standards which may be conveniently adjusted
to suit the fashions of the times.

Adherents to this new viewpoint find it advantageous to
describe our social ills in terms of young versus old. This
attitude presents the conflict as one between glamorous, vital
youth and stodgy middle age. In reality, we will discover that
the self-described "generation gap" is a *morality* gap. It is a
schism between two value systems, one of which seeks to
replace the other.

While advocates of flexible morality are offering us the
deceptively appealing youth culture, they are simultaneously
suggesting that there are no such things as basic right and
wrong, and evil. They also challenge us on the more superficial levels of taste, style, manners and customs. The

gauntlet has been thrown down. Are those of us who believe in a more traditional sense of morality ready to face the challenge?

The picture is not entirely bleak; just as Alice left the Mad Tea Party and returned to a world of rational beings, so can we still escape the political jungle and cultural vacuum offered by the youth cult. We shall see that the "old" values do work and are valid. If they have not created the perfect society, it is because man is imperfect. In our imperfection, we do not always behave according to our professed principles and ideals. Young America is by no means homogeneous in its taste or outlook. This is the view of a segment of young America that has been silenced because a benevolent élite of college professors, politicians, pseudo-intellectuals, and "thinkers" have chosen to ignore it.

The 1960's were years of harsh and destructive change for this country. The 1970's offer a challenge; we can recognize the counterculture and its intellectual offspring, the youth cult, as an aberration, and we can revitalize our institutions and principles, or we can watch our society fall apart. The choice is ours.

II.

"ROCK" IS A FOUR-LETTER WORD!

Success has a great tendency to conceal and throw a veil over the evil deeds of men . . . . .Demosthenes

The superior man understands what is right; the inferior man understands what will sell . . . . .Confucius

If any single medium of expression could be said to represent the youth culture in the mind of the general public, it is "rock," a term established through truncated use of "rock and roll," the popular teenage dance music that has suddenly assumed a role of social significance in our daily lives.

It is impossible to escape rock, should one desire to do so. It is on television, on radio, on record. Rock groups may be heard at the most élite parties of the wealthy and socially prominent who are described as "beautiful people"; they also may be heard at your high-school game.

What is this phenomenon, described by one observer as a "protean music capable of almost limitless expression? " On the surface, at least, eminently respectable! Leaders of rock groups are rich and famous. The most famous group, the Beatles, was decorated by the Queen of England. A national organization of music teachers has advocated introducing rock in the school system, and one of the most bizarre group leaders has been invited to lecture at an old and widely regarded university. Rock groups have appeared in concert with symphony orchestras, to the delight of such conductors as Leonard Bernstein and Zubin Mehta, and have been welcomed into the homes and parties of the status-conscious literary circles, with the full approval of the latter's social arbiter, Truman Capote. Rock music is criticized with a reverence formerly reserved only for the nation's most distinguished concert music. All in all, rock music seems respectable.

In a day and age when it is fashionable to ridicule the flag, and motherhood is subject to the daily tirades of women's liberationists, rock music has become something of a sacred cow. The critical observer who reaches for his earplugs when the electric guitars are plugged in and the amplifiers are turned up is asking for trouble.

But we have already dared to rush in where angels and music critics alike fear to tread and will soon discover some surprising truths about the rock-music phenomenon. Some of these truths relate to music, some to morals, and all to money. Ultimately, they will reveal the massive fraud that has been perpetrated upon society, aided and abetted by those citizens whose fear of being called "old-fashioned" has caused them to check their common sense (and their eardrums) at the nearest rock-concert ticket window.

From the beginning, rock music has grown through the interaction of two elements: teenage rebellion and fast-talking promoters. The managers responsible for creating the rock phenomenon are not unlike used-car salesmen. Success or failure is measured as much by the manager as by the performers themselves. The Beatles, four young Englishmen in their twenties, living in Liverpool, began an early phase of their careers under the management of an over-thirty nightclub owner, Allan Williams. "I couldn't have done what Brian Epstein did for them," admitted Williams, "nor what he did for Gerry and the Pacemakers." In a reference to Brian Epstein, Williams was acknowledging what most middle-aged apologists for rock refuse to recognize as even in existence: the commercial fraternity of rock promoter-

managers who are personally responsible for the billion dollar industry with all its ramifications. For Brian Epstein, like
Colonel Tom Parker before him, was responsible for manag-
ing and manipulating the careers of pop-music idols. What
has this to do with the "profound philosophical revolution"
associated with the counterculture? Nothing, and this is
precisely the point. A brief examination of the history of
rock (as seen by those familiar with the London, New York,
Hollywood, and Nashville recording industries) reveals that
the initial origins of rock were anything but sociological. Bill
Haley was one of the first rock stars, and some teenagers
who saw his film, *Rock Around the Clock*, when it was released in 1956, responded by tearing up the theater. The
event was, in some ways, prophetic. Although proponents of
rock music preach "peace" in their public relations communications, the phenomenon has always been associated with
the frustrations of teenagers. In the 1950's, this rebellion
was turned against forms of authority: parents, school, and
restrictions of any kind. But in the 1960's, combined with
the drug culture and egged on by violent political revolutionaries, the rebellion took an even uglier turn. Haley was
soon eclipsed by another star, a young man named Elvis
Presley.

Elvis Presley, generally considered to be the superstar of
the rock world, began his career around the Nashville radio
stations.

Curiously enough, Presley still considered himself a
country-western singer during this period. Presley's rock
career improved, however, when he came under the guidance
of the incredible Colonel Tom Parker. Who was Parker?
Stanley Booth, writing in *Esquire*, provides the answer:
"Thomas Andrew Parker, a latter-day Barnum out of W.C.
Fields by William Burroughs. A carnival orphan, he had
worked in his uncle's 'Great Parker Pony Circus,' dipped can-
died apples, shaved ice for snow cones, operated merry-go-
rounds, even put in a stretch as a dog catcher in Tampa,
Florida." But Parker was not a man to be held down by the
fortunes of life. Soon Presley was appearing on the "Ed
Sullivan Show," earning $50,000 for three appearances.

When Presley returned home, Parker arranged for him to appear at a charity benefit. After three hours of waiting for other performers to finish their acts, the audience finally got to see Presley, who proceeded, according to Stanley Booth, to simulate sexual intercourse with the microphone.

If Presley's gyrations upset the mothers of America, off stage and off camera he was reputed to behave like a gentleman. He addressed his employers in the recording industry as "Sir," or "Ma'am." Presley thus offset his onstage antics with an ingenuous private image. If this made his performance more respectable, some observers were not fooled. Unlike the singing idols of the 1940's, particularly Frank Sinatra, Presley did not sing about romance or moonlight or sing the poetic lyrics of Oscar Hammerstein, According to rock historian Nik Cohn, the teenage girls who screamed at Presley's concerts had no time for sighing, swooning, and sobbing. He recalls, "With rock though, it's all been down to mainline sexual fantasy. Sitting in concert halls, school girls have screamed, rioted, brawled, and fainted. They've wet themselves and they've masturbated. According to P. J. Proby, they've even ripped the legs off their chairs and mauled themselves. They've done all kinds of outrageous stuff they'd never do anywhere else, and they've been so uninhibited because there has always been a safety belt, because the pop singer himself has been unreachable, unreal, and nothing could actually happen." Nor had the situation changed by the late 1960's, when Cohn reportedly became bored with the viciousness of the Rolling Stones after a concert and returned to the deserted auditorium. He reported again that "the small girls had screamed too hard and wet themselves. Not just one or two of them, but many, so that the floor was sodden and the stench was overwhelming."

The use of a rock concert as a sexual stimulant was the beginning; the end was the Roman orgy, contemporary style, with bell-bottoms replacing togas, and packaged under the label of Woodstock. The mothers who feared for their daughters' morality in the 1950's were not unjustified. A recent article by Sam Sutherland, writing in *Penthouse*, declares, "In the early 1970's it has come to pass that rock' n'roll appears to have revealed itself as precisely what mom and dad feared it might be: sex."

The rock stars who followed Presley were of many varieties. Each had his own particular image, carefully molded by his manager, with clothing, life-style, and personality designed to follow the trends. Screamin' Jay Hawkins, whose career began back in the 1940's, emerged flaming from a coffin, carrying a smoking skull. Little Richard pounded the piano keyboard with the heel of his foot. Jerry Lee Lewis virtually attacked the piano with his feet and fists, and finally closed his act by jumping on top of the piano. The trends changed. Rock songs began emphasizing the youth culture that existed in high-school. Political revolutionaries hadn't yet gained an influence on the high school campus, and life seemed to be a continuous array of dates, cokes, hamburgers, french fries, parties, and music. The boys wore crew cuts, the girls pony-tails. Parents were "square," but they'd come around, eventually. Rock songs talked about lipstick, love, dating, being sweet sixteen, girl friends, and boy friends. The trends changed again. The record promoters tried the "Twist," a dancing fad from the Peppermint Lounge in New York, which became fashionable. This time, not only the teenagers but the rich and famous middle-aged adults tried "twisting." Chubby Checker, a former chicken plucker from Philadelphia, recorded the tune, "Let's Twist Again," a revival of an old rock song. Checker became the subject of a variety of promotions ranging from the Chubby Checker T-shirts to Chubby Checker dolls. The twist was eventually replaced by a variety of dances, all performed alone; none of the dances were related to the partnership of a couple dancing (or romancing) together. The dances changed, the names changed, and somehow remained the same: loud, noisy, and full of sexual display. The Beach Boys sang about surfing and hotrods, and both activites seemed preferable to homework in the minds of teenage boys.

The ultimate pop explosion came in the mid-1960's, in England, with the advent of the Beatles. Their rise has been chronicled in every possible medium, but little attention has been focused on the machinations of their manager, Brian

Epstein. In the early days of their career, the Beatles were tough, greasy, lower-class pop musicians with few artistic pretensions. By the time Epstein had finished, they were undoubtedly the four most well-known young men in the world and for the millions of pounds they brought into England, the Queen gave them the M.B.E.

The Beatles, formerly an unsuccesful skifflc band in Liverpool, discovered their amplified sound in Germany, where, out of money, they could only afford two amplifiers for their four guitars. Paul McCartney declared, "We didn't worry about arrangements or anything. If we had trouble with our overworked amplifiers — we had to plug two guitars into one — I'd just chuck everything in and start leaping around the stage or rush to the piano and start playing some chords . . . it was noise and beat all the way."

Epstein, a twenty-six-year-old Englishman, set out to manage the Beatles as Parker had managed Elvis Presley. Far from being the unique, spontaneous art form which resulted from a groundswell of sympathy and creative energy in the soul of America (or England), rock was initially and always a stylistic commodity which proved unsuccessful until managed by ambitious businessmen. Some of the managers, were as bizarre as the acts they promoted. Nik Cohn described the typical agent or record producer in these terms: "He hated pop but liked money. He was also often homosexual, and since his job lay mostly in discovering pretty young boys, this helped. He found the act he wanted and made a record. This record was then released, and either it sold or it was hyped.

One of the most successful of all rock promoters, who prefers to remain anonymous, admitted to the author "I've made stars of untalented people; I did it for the money." Another of these manager-tycoons maintains an office on the Sunset Strip which is decorated entirely in expensive antiques.

The rock movement did not begin simultaneously with the influx of political radicalism on the campuses. The pop-record industry, absorbing an interest in surfing or beach parties or whatever happened to be the latest teenage fad,

was equally ready to espouse political radicalism if the latter
proved profitable.

The true nature of the record industry may be seen by
those who ignore the superficial aura of glamor which seems
to surround persons employed in the entertainment fields.
Paul Ackerman, editor of *Billboard* (the bible of the record
industry, because it enables record executives to see who has
earned the most money), testified in Congressional hearings
that payola (bribes used by record executives or their representatives to monopolize broadcast time with emphasis on
"plugging" selected recordings) was standard procedure in
the recording industry.

Recently, former Capitol Records executive, Roger Karshner, shocked the public with a new book, *The Music Machine*, in which he told about the record industry. Karshner
describes an incredible world of phonies, phony billings,
phony charts, phony trends, and mediocrity, stimulated by
"payola, layola, flyola," and other forms of bribery and
chicanery. He indicates that mass prostitution is a common
inducement used at recording industry sales conventions, and
recounts numerous incidents of stardom for untalented
"musicians" who became overnight "superstars" and "country-western" performers who have seen neither the country
nor the West. He also discusses "untalented megalomaniacs"
who dominate the industry who speak only of "dynamic
success," "dynamic sales," and dynamic superstars," while
those truly endowed with talent or abilities are often sent
begging. A pop musician whose managerial backers are able
to find a successful promotional technique for their client
may suddenly be recognized as a "creative genius."

While musicians of a variety of tastes and levels are suffering nervous collapse en masse, for fear that someone will
render them "obsolete" for failing to recognize the validity
of "rock," the publicity machines continue to function.

Karshner comments, "Now the musical 'meat packers' go
to work. The local sales organization orders voluminous
quantities of the record to 'cover' the market in anticipation
of consumer demands created by jingle-jangle radio. The
record is shipped to every dealer, every rack jobber, and

every one-stop. Stacks and racks of the record loom like black smokestacks on retail counters all over the city. The company is ready, prepared, armed; every salesman becomes a veritable wholesale minuteman prepared to die of absurdity." Karshner has courageously revealed what others refuse to admit, except in private.

As for the "social motivation" of "superstars," Karshner describes a typical example: a rich and influential young man who moves into an East Village apartment discovers the "social injustice" of being poor, and emerges as a protest singer. As the young man is promoted and publicized, he becomes a "superstar" who identifies with the oppressed and exploited. Ultimately, he identifies so much with these people that he learns to "hate" his country estate, his new Rolls Royce, his private airplane, his new home overlooking the ocean, and all the material possessions he regularly acquired. Most of all, he "hated" the millions of dollars he continued to earn, and of course, he "hated" society, businessmen, the government, the police, and everyone else.

Karshner also succeeded in recognizing much of the hypocrisy present in the recording industry. He decided to tell the truth about the new image which many of today's current record producers seek to project. He says, "There are many young people in publishing also. They're regaled in the latest garb of hippydom, peeking from behind scruffly hair with cool eyes. They look right, talk softly, and hasten to tell you that their "heads are together" and that their aim is on the creative target of free artistic expression. But underneath the Mickey Mouse T-shirts and behind the patches on the old Levis lies lurking little bald, overdressed, bent-over greedy-fingered midgets with cigar stained Masonic rings . . . and the markets are flooded and consumers are besieged with the oversold, overmerchandised, overadvertised dregs that are the residue of the big lie. . ."

Karshner is not alone in recognizing the hollow spirits of these individuals. Nik Cohn commented, "Where the way to break the bubblegum market is simply to shout, to be louder and flashier and more vulgar than the competition, the avant-garde has to be breached by stealth, by intellectual flattery, by the suggestion that only the very finest minds can understand the product offered. On that basis, though, the intelligentsia is possibly even more gullible than the kids." The noted poet Karl Shapiro remarked, "The wave of male and female hysterics with guitars and brotherhood lyrics turned into a mass industry on one hand and on the other, a generation of revoltés without goals." Finally, Ernest Hemmingway, hardly an unsophisticated observer, summed up that whole matter He said, "We are deluged with writers who can't write, actors who can't act, singers who can't sing . . . and they are all making a million dollars a year."

These matters may be of no interest to those who prefer to dwell on the "aesthetics" of rock. But such critics should remember that not one single rock song or lyric has been recorded without achieving in some measure the approval of these recording executives, and that anyone cognizant of the penthouse offices of New York rock promoters (or the Sunset Strip – Beverly Hills counterparts) is aware that these men regard themselves in private as "image-builders" capable of making any idea (or philosophical attitude) or any star "commercial" by cranking up the wheels of their multibillion dollar publicity machines. Those who talk about the spontaneity of rock blithely ignore the fact that many rock groups are not signed to record contracts. This is not because they are less cognizant of the cohesive revolution he desires to portray, but because the powers that be which dominate the promotion and management in this field have not decided that their efforts should be made in behalf of these particular groups. If well-educated men want to persuade themselves or the public that the rise of any specific movement in rock is the result of ideological or stylistic timeliness, it's fine with the promoters. What does a former rock idol say about himself now that his career is in a stage of development in which he can afford to be honest? Fabian Forte, once known as "The Fabulous Fabian," says, "I could carry a tune, but that's about all. The rest was just ballyhoo."

First, we are reminded that the rock groups exude "boundless energy." The music is amplified electronically, sometimes to such a decibel level that the words cannot be understood and the music becomes a deafening drone. This becomes rock's "complex texture." Rock groups are characterized as small cells of universal brotherhood in which young people participate, like Renaissance men, as composers. One inevitable bond between the rock group or soloist and the audience is that both presumably have taken drugs as an integral part of the musical experience. The groups live or work together in a commune, expressing their own "unique personalities." If they worked at any point in their careers in a discotheque, their performances are characterized as "multimedia experiences." The various media involved presumably include sex and drugs as well as the music. Finally, the lyrics are presented as a manifestation of poetry, a poignant effort to be heard amid the chaos and confusion that dominates the rest of the world.

A prime example of this disdain for money is a young man named James Brown. Brown, is a soul singer. He expresses the role of the black man in rock, but his works are intended to be understood by persons of all races, especially those who identify with poverty and humility.

James Brown, widely recognized as the most successful "soul" singer, is a case in point. Brown, a spokesman for the poor and disenfranchised, travels with a uniformed chauffeur. He has a three-car garage, a purple Cadillac limousine, a red Stingray with "Mr. Dynamite" painted on the side, and a white Cadillac. Brown has been known to use 1000 pairs of cufflinks a month, which he tosses to the audience during his performances. His wardrobe consists of 120 glistening shirts, slacks, capes, and eighty pairs of shoes and boots. He is surrounded by a managerial staff that attends to his needs. On tour, he is preceded by a team of interior decorators who redesign the hotel rooms he will occupy, especially to suit his taste. Once, James Brown was very poor. Now, however, he leads a life-style which some believe is irreverent in regard to money. Protest is profitable in the 1970's.

It is easy enough to declare that the philosophies of the rock stars as expressed in their lyrics may differ with the attitudes exemplified by their life-styles. But if this is true,

they are hypocrites and should be treated accordingly. Nik
Cohn recalled a conversation with Bert Berns, an active pop
songwriter. He asked Berns to explain what pop was about.
Berns responded by turning around, and summoning a waiter
to their table. Cohn commented, "Immediately, three waiters
burst out of the wings at a canter and dashed to our table.
Berns asked for a match and was faced by a sudden wall of
flame, by three flickering hands. When the waiters left, Berns
looked at me and wasn't even smug about it. 'Wouldn't you
say?' he asked, 'That's what pop's about.'"

Mick Jagger, leader of the Rolling Stones, who has an
irreverent perspective on the subject of financial profit, is
known to maintain a dark blue Aston Martin, an eleven-
bedroom house in Hampshire with butler's cottage and man-
made lake, and a town house in Chelsea. The former is
evaluated at £25,000 and the latter at £45,000. Elvis Presley
lives on an estate in Tennessee large enough to accommodate
indoor roller skating. The list is endless. A record company
called Coed Records went to Federal Court, proposing that
payola should be a legalized business exemption on income
tax. If the "myth" of "irreverence toward money" helps to
build an anti-Establishment image, all to the good, so far as
the rock-promoters are concerned. But the rock groups never
forget that a major publication devoted to their efforts is
appropriately named, Cashbox. This is really tracing rock to
its roots.

The intellectuals' embrace of the counterculture in general, and rock in particular, was predictable, and lost no time
in coming. A Yale Professor of Law, Charles Reich, wrote a
book called The Greening of America. Reich's best-selling
book, was hailed by school teachers, parents, and well-meaning adults of all ages who wrote to Reich, thanking him for
explaining that the kids were really all right after all.

Reich's thesis was essentially that conservatives were
trying to turn the clock back in opposition to change, that
liberals were busy trying to change the world through institutions, and that only the young people would be successful
because they would start a peaceful, non-violent cultural
revolution. This revolution, we were told, would come about

only through individual conversion, rather than through violent change. Reich then proceeded to write long apologia for the youth cult, slobbism, rock music, and the drug culture. He assigned impressive labels to the conservatives (Consciousness I), liberals (Consciousness II), and revolutionaries, peaceful or otherwise (Consciousness III). But Reich's ideal social unit turned out to be the commune, his celebration of life, the rock festival, his model form of municipal cooperation, the co-op supermarket at Berkeley. The rock festival is approximately as peaceful in a tranquil community as a herd of stampeding elephants downtown at rush hour. The squalor, filth, and blatant immorality of the Berkeley radicals does not speak well for Consciousness III. Although Reich tried to give the revolution respectability, his arguments were devoid of logic, and ultimately, instead of raising the level of the dropout culture, he inadvertently exposed its weaknesses, as well as those of some of the faculty members of our universities.

We now turn to consideration of the life-style of these rock groups, a life-style with which young persons who have achieved Charles Reich's Consciousness III are expected to sympathize.

Reich suggests that "the use of drugs, especially because they are illegal, establishes a blood brotherhood before the musicians even begin to play." The same could be said for holding up a bank or committing other assorted crimes. Imagine the outrage heard from the public if a respected social critic were to suggest that a troupe of actors or dancers establish a blood brotherhood by burning all existing copies of *The Greening of America*. While this might be considered a public service in some circles, it seems logical that thoughtful, sensible Americans would oppose such actions as illegal and immoral; it would seem that they would oppose a blood brotherhood based on violation of the drug laws for the same reasons. Perhaps Charles Reich would agree, but he does not choose to tell us.

John Lennon, who modestly asserted that the Beatles were more popular than Jesus, has offered a description of the Beatles' life-style at the height of their success.

"The Beatles tours were like the Fellini film *Satirycon*," he declared, acknowledging free use of girls, marijuana, LSD, and heroin. "Wherever we went, there was always a whole scene going, we had four separate bedrooms." When pressed by a reporter as to how the group managed to keep its "clean image" during these tours, which he freely compared to Roman orgies, Lennon replied, "Everybody wants to keep on the bandwagon of free women, liquor and fun." Is this the idealistic life-style based on a new sense of values publicized by the apologists for rock groups? In truth, these values are no different from the values which dominate any corrupt society.

John Lennon is not unique among the Beatles in this respect, just as the Beatles are not unique among rock groups. These young men and women, projected into positions of importance and wealth far beyond their achievements, receive the adoration of the masses. Like wolves in sheep's clothing, they enjoy the advantages and pleasures of an amoral existence while chastising conservative society as a social conscience. Their promiscuous, irresponsible life-style is based on instant gratification; they cannot fail to serve their whims, because the usual values which affect the lives of stronger men are irrelevant to their material existences. Like spoiled children, they indulge themselves, while their middle-aged press agents (and academic apologists) applaud their discovery of a life-style that is as old as corruption itself, and as morally jaded.

Some also suggest the rock group as the ideal example of cooperative brotherhood. This, of course, is utter nonsense, as anyone vaguely familiar with the legal relationships between group members will affirm. Paul McCartney went to court to have the Beatles legally dissolved; McCartney also asked the courts to appoint financial managers to take control of the money earned by the Beatles during the years they were enjoying their spirit of brotherhood for fun and profit. Lennon, not to be outdone, insisted that he, not McCartney, had been the first to abandon the group.

Most of the Beatles' legal problems are not unique, however. Many of the rock groups engage in various kinds of legal intrigues. Often it is because one member of the group, like the Supremes' Diana Ross, is ambitious enough to try to become a superstar on her own. The rock groups sue their managers; they often sue each other. Recently, a prominent Hollywood manager, preferring to remain anonymous, recalled a friend of his, a San Francisco promoter, who experienced some of the brotherhood of the rock groups. He found a group of nomadic youngsters in the Haight-Ashbury section of San Francisco. The manager bought them a group of musical instruments, taught them elementary guitar chords, because they were musically illiterate, purchased costumes, paid their rent, and went to work promoting a public image. The group, exemplifying the spirit of brotherhood described by rock-music critics, promptly took their manager to court. They sued and won.

In the 1960's, the nature of pop-music lyrics changed radically. The early rock lyrics had been derivative of country-and-western subjects (i.e., Presley's "Hound Dog") and scaled the heights of teenage inanity with the Beatles' "I Want to Hold Your Hand." Gradually, however, pop music began to absorb those influences of the high school and college cultures which were growing like giant weeds. A high school coed would hardly worry about being sweet sixteen if she were primarily concerned about her alleged right to get an abortion. Crew-cuts and football had been replaced by the "right" to take LSD. The youth cult, with its emphasis on free love (or more appropriately, free sex), drugs, and revolution, was making itself heard. Bob Dylan became a well-known figure in pop music, and the Beatles started turning to social and political subjects. For the first time, rock music and lyrics were acquiring artistic pretensions. Previously, the total lack of quality, the obvious bad music and bad lyrics, had been a selling point to teenage audiences. A curious interaction between pop musicians and journalists came into play. The journalists were eager to advance their own theories about Vietnam, abortion, drugs, long hair, and a variety of social issues. The presence of influential and very rich songwriters who trumpeted their own views was convenient. Advocates of the counterculture could point to the

success of "rock music" with its protest lyrics as a justification for their own political programs, candidates, and
ambitions. The rock groups (and their promoters) could
draw upon critical acclaim as a publicity device.

Eager to find the "poignant, eloquent voices of youthful
protest" which the journalists and pseudo-intellectuals decided had to be found somewhere in the younger generation,
they turned to the rock groups. If the music was unmusical,
if the lyrics were crude, no matter—not so long as the social
and political views matched their own interpretation of the
political events at hand. The result was an almost comical
situation; the rock composers and lyricists were credited
with the most unbelievable political and social profundity.
The "intellectuals" echoed the views of the rock groups who
echoed the views of the intellectuals.

The journalists and professors, eager to reinforce their
own preconceived notions about the younger generation,
conveniently neglected those young men and women who
did not subscribe to the social or political views espoused by
the rock groups. Instead, they waited eagerly for the rock
composers and lyricists, now armed with their new-found
academic respectability, to sit down in their elegant man-
sions, set aside their furs, jewels, and Rolls-Royces, and write
the weekly protest.

But rock music and lyrics had never before been accepted
as anything but teenage music. Now the counterculture was
offering its self-styled "philosophy" as the viewpoint of the
younger generation. Even high school newspapers had become involved in controversies over the alleged "right" to
take drugs or to print obscenities in school publications.
Gradually, publishers and record companies became more
and more permissive, welcoming each new four-letter word
or suggestive reference to drugs or sex in the lyrics as a
crusade. Suddenly the record industry, like an intoxicated
octopus, began the inevitable search to find something more
shocking or controversial than ever before. It didn't have to
look very far.

Rock music had always attracted the strange and bizarre;
it was one of the few fields of endeavor in which one could

become a superstar, with all the trappings of fame and wealth, without any special talents or skills, save the ability to choose the right manager. A careful study of the lyrics of hit songs reveals no special insights; rather, we find lyrics which happened to be on the right (or should we say *left*) side of the political fence.

The ultimate philosophical statement of the counter-culture was supposed to be the American tribal love-rock musical, *Hair*. Written by Gerome Ragni and James Rado, and produced under the auspices of Joseph Papp, *Hair* had something for everyone. By wrapping itself in the mantle of youth, *Hair* could glory in its amateurism and eschew any claims of professionalism. *Hair* was promoted as a celebration, a show full of love, the best that the young people of this country had to offer. The lyrics, admittedly, were primitive, but the critics wanted to be understanding. The kids, we were told, meant well, as they sang, "Let it fly in the breeze and get caught in the trees, give a home to the fleas in my hair."

Hair had no plot, in the sense of a formal book-musical. Instead, it consisted of a deafening, amplified revue of rock songs, a cast kept constantly in motion, writhing and twisting to the music. A loosely constructed story-line about a young man named "Claude" tied the songs together. Claude, it seems, had been drafted, and the prospect of giving up all he held dearly, most especially his flea-infested hair, a ready supply of marijuana, the right to swear in mixed company, and a girl friend who believed in free and easy sex, was too much to bear. *Hair* gloried in its primitive crudity, virtually daring the critics to dislike it. Realistically, it should have been received as a poorly conceived musical, with no book, ineffectively crude lyrics, and non-music. Instead, the critics purred. Clive Barnes, writing in the *New York Times*, called the show, "Sweet, subtle, and sheer fun." Much of the attention focused on a scene in which members of the cast, wearing absolutely nothing, at all, faced the audience on a dimly lighted stage. Critical reaction varied. One observer said that when nudity came to Broadway, "All those Scarsdale ladies got to look at a **strange man's** bottom."

Hair offered the youth cult and portrayed it exactly as it really is: dirty, crude, vulgar, and concerned primarily with sex, drugs, indulgence, and self-gratification.

If the Beatles' long hair seemed effeminate to the men who wore crew-cuts in the 1950's, the new groups would go one step farther.

The result has not been a coherent political or social philosophy, or even a set of skillfully written lyrics or musically inspired tunes. Instead, society has been offered a freak show. Michel Polnareff, a French pop-singer, appears in a woman's hat, frilly blouse, with his own backside bare. An advertisement for the Edgar Winter Group pictured a person with alabaster skin, white hair, dark lipstick, bare shoulders, and a silver necklace. Nationally syndicated columnist, Art Seidenbaum, remarked, "Only the prominent Adam's apple suggested that this mysterious creature is a man." Seidenbaum also refers to rock-star, David Bowie, as, "an artist of imprecise sex who deliberately blurs the fine line between that which is male and that which is female."

In recent months, rock audiences have become so accustomed to the sick, the bizarre, the violent, and the obscene, that promoters are forced to seek new depths of depravity in order to hit the Top Forty. By catering to the most abnormal elements of a society, businessmen can always find some new curiosity to be advertised as a thrill. But they offer us a sick, violent, obscene exhibition, not the idyllic wholesome, expression of "America's young people," that slick salesmen would have us believe.

In today's culture, rock is taken seriously. It is reviewed in magazines that are considered "intellectual fare." Universities offer courses in rock music. Wiley Housewright, former President of the Music Educators National Conference, has urged that rock be introduced in the public schools as a means of "communication" with students of elementary school age.

What are the aesthetics of rock? For an answer, it is best to turn to primary sources, the young men and women who create rock themselves. Frank Zappa is the leader of a musical aggregation known as the Mothers of Invention. Because he has attended college, he is generally accepted as one of the aesthetic spokesmen of the rock movement; in any event, he is advertised as such. Zappa likes to suggest that he is a satirist. He is ridiculing society, and trying to take an ironic view of life in general, including the youth culture. But Zappa went so far as to produce an album entitled "We're Only in it for the Money." Perhaps the academic apologists deserve Zappa, but unfortunately, the rest of society must tolerate his creative efforts as well. Zappa demonstrated his capacity to be the spokesman for the aesthetics of rock when he had himself photographed sitting on the toilet.

Zappa explained to Sally Kempton the aesthetic background of the group: "We were playing at local beer joints for like six dollars a night. I finally decided this would not do, so I began calling up all the clubs in the area. This was in 1965, and to get work you had to sound like the Beatles and Rolling Stones." (Observe the anti-Establishment Beatles and Stones who had everyone against them!) Zappa goes on. "You also had to have long hair and due to an unfortunate circumstance all my hair had been cut off. I used to tell club managers that we sounded exactly like the Rolling Stones. Anyway we finally got a booking in a club in Pomona, and were something of a hit. It was more because of our act than because of our music. People used to go away and tell their friends that here was this group that insulted the audience." (It is easy to see why Frank Zappa grew long hair; he obviously wanted to be a "non-conformist.")

Zappa's efforts prevailed. "Then MGM sent someone around to sign us to a contract. Their guy came into the club during a set of 'Brain Police' and he said, 'Aha, a protest rhythm and blues group,' so they paid us accordingly. The fee we got for singing was incredibly small, particularly considering the number of guys in the group."

We see no sense of bitter social protest, no sense of ideological outrage, no sense of passionate desires to break with the established goals of society. What we see, as expressed in the words of a leading member of the musical movement

described by many as our new cultural, social conscience is
that Frank Zappa wanted to make money, to be successful
(in the conventional, materialistic sense). Social protest was
considered to be commercially viable by the commercial
promoters, and Frank Zappa was happy to oblige.

Zappa's career rose steadily; he now runs his own advertising agency, which presumably helped to publicize a concert which featured the Mothers of Invention and the Los
Angeles Philharmonic in a work especially written by Zappa,
to be conducted by the regular symphony musical director,
Zubin Nehta. The site of this concert was Pauley Pavilion,
home of the UCLA basketball dynasty. To make the concert
respectable, the Philharmonic also added a new electronic
composition written for orchestra and tape recorder by Mel
Powell, of Yale, the 1940's dance bands, and now Dean of
the School of Music at California Institute of the Arts.
Powell, after a technical breakdown resulting from a faulty
cable prevented completion of the performance of his piece,
decided that his work could not receive serious attention. He
tried to leave the auditorium, declining another attempt at
performance because Zappa's group had taken over the stage.
His exit was blocked by the mercurial Ernest Fleischmann,
manager and executive director of the Philharmonic. When
he saw that Powell was determined to leave the auditorium,
Fleischmann responded by promising that Powell would
never again receive a performance of his work by the Philharmonic. Powell, justifiably furious, struck home in his
denunciation of the pseudo-intellectual rationale employed
by apologists for much of today's current pop music. He
also explained the rapport, the feeling of kindred spirit that
exists between rock groups and their audiences.

Powell declares: "Minimal musical awareness informs us
that there isn't an instrumental, vocal, or compositional
entity presented nowadays by the majority of rock groups to
their millions of devotees that is so much as an inch beyond
the reach of an utterly unaccomplished amateur. Except for
the handful of genuinely gifted in this field, its profession
becomes a form of participatory democracy in which the
talentless kid in his living room plunking away on his guitar

idolizes the equally talentless kid on the tube or recording, plunking away on his guitar. If the medium is the message, the message here is that the medium is an ego trip mirror; it scarcely matters who is transmitting, who is receiving." Powell has correctly identified the dangers of applying egalitarian attitudes to evaluation of the arts.

"Doing one's own thing" has become a convenient excuse for a lack of creative talent or imagination. Because pop music is offered as "people's music," we seem almost eager to excuse the fact that the performers have little to offer. It may be very well for a performer to simply "do his own thing" but if he's doing it on national television or in Carnegie Hall, one hopes he is capable of carrying a tune or playing more that five chords on his guitar.

The result is the usual obliteration of values and debunking of excellence which has become the curse of the glorified youth culture. Powell observes, "The rule then becomes either Beethoven was black or he wasn't beautiful. Mozart does his thing, and so does Ringo. Man it's the same, don't you dig? Bach and those cats got their own scene just like Snooty Sam and the Father-Grabbing Anti-Oinkers got their own scene." Powell concludes with the comment, "An immediate consequence of this conceptual garbage is the commercial exploitation of genuinely well-intentioned young innocents whose deep devotion to social justice somehow renders them so vulnerable to music-hustling demagogues." What Powell has realized, and what others do not, is that intelligent, well-meaning people, in their desire to bend over backward to be receptive to creative work which is advertised as youth-oriented, may check their common sense (and their taste, if they have any) at the door when they try to evaluate rock concerts. Zappa, explaining some of his aesthetic ideas, recalls, "It was very tough getting the group together in the beginning. A lot of guys didn't want to submit to our packaging. They didn't like making themselves ugly, but they especially didn't like playing ugly." Zappa's techniques of orchestration are unusual to say the least. "I found some violins in a closet and I gave them to three of the guys. None of them had ever played a violin before. They were making all these weird sounds on them."

It is common knowledge in the music industry that a guitar, knowledge of a few chords, and a gullible, willing public, are enough to create rock stars if the manager or promoter does his job. Of course, it is always advisable to prepackage such performing artists, employing a publicity campaign. Ideally, they should claim to express profound aesthetic meanings in their work, fashionably related to the popular political trends of the day. Critics, academics, and some of the public like to think that rock is treated as a serious art form. Pontification and pretentiousness are customarily greeted with glee.

Frank Zappa, advertising executive in behalf of his own work, expressed amusement that MGM Records objected to certain lyrics of his which the company felt could be interpreted as obscene. Zappa's response was to indicate that war and other public ills were his idea of bad taste.

This is a classic case of *non sequitur*. Why does the existence of social ills justify bad taste or obscenity, on the part of Zappa or anyone else? Zappa, of course, can defend himself by saying that standards of taste and obscenity are relative. The concept of shifting, relative standards is fashionable today, because cultural anarchy thrives on the notion that there are no fixed standards of taste or beauty. Although individual styles have varied for years among composers, writers, and artists, great masterworks of art have exhibited certain common traits that overlap the beginnings and endings of eras. (In music, the capacity to write beautiful melody is a case in point.)

One standard objection to criticism of rock groups is the assertion that closed minds (or ears) may overlook the work of a neglected genius. Critics inevitably remind us of Eduard Hanslick, the musical reviewer who ridiculed the innovations of Wagner in the late nineteenth century. Like all reasonable principles, openmindedness can be carried too far. At one time, courts handed down harsh sentences; today, many Americans believe that the courts are permissive and inclined to favor the criminal. A similar situation exists in music.

Certain critics are so afraid of failing to recognize another Wagner that they may accept a performer who bangs two tin cans together as a virtuoso. The poet who mumbles incoherently or shouts obscenities at an audience is accepted because the critics are afraid of becoming known as the men who failed to identify another Keats.

Another familiar argument raised suggests that a performance by a contemporary musician or singer must be judged within its own context. But this too can lead us astray; if the large majority of such performers cannot sing or play well, the untalented mediocrity is elevated to star status because he is compared with his even less talented rivals.

The concept of uniform standards does not propose our evaluation of contemporary art by antiquated standards. But we can be careful enough not to create an elite class of artists whose work cannot be criticized, under the sanctuary of a modern label. Bad musicianship and incoherence cannot be overlooked in the works of self-styled modernists, especially when these standards are applied to everyone else.

Critics try to analyze and explain the lyrics of rock groups as "poetry." Unfortunately, middle-aged apologists for the rock culture blithely assume that rock lyrics are profound. Yet the widely criticized "Sergeant Pepper," analyzed by all the major critics and commentators, is a prime example of what is wrong with intellectual rock criticism. Paul McCartney describes the choice of title in these words: "I was just thinking of nice words like 'Sergeant Pepper and Lonely Hearts Club,' and they came together for no reason." The poetry which critics praise espouses the political and social attitudes of the self-styled cultural revolution. We shall shortly examine some of these attitudes to determine whether or not they are really profound. Perhaps a prime example of this philosophy is the lyric by the Jefferson Airplane, that declares, "We are obscene, lawless, hideous, dangerous, dirty, violent, and young." These revolutionary lyrics also inform us, "We are all outlaws in the eyes of Amerika. In order to survive, we steal, cheat, lie, forge, _____ hide and deal." (Obscenity not printed.)

The Rolling Stones sing, "The time is ripe for violent revolution." John Coyne suggests, "Visit Berkeley and look at the kids, the young ones. Junior-high-school girls with eyes as knowing and dead as any prostitute's. They've had it all, they know things at thirteen that we didn't learn until our twenties. They've experienced it all, years before they were mentally ready, and by the late teens they're jaded. They never will get any satisfaction, for they've experienced it before they should, and when they reach the age at which they're mentally ready, it's behind them."

Surprisingly enough, the most curious reaction to the efforts of these groups has come from middle-class and affluent Americans. Rock is socially "in." We can hear it at the best parties. Some of our most famous musical figures have endorsed it as a serious art form.

To understand this, we must remember that the culture revolution which has occurred at a lightning-fast pace has affected adults as well as children. When we speak of rock as the music of the "young," we must remember that many of these "youngsters" are over thirty. Society is fashionable for the young. Like Br'er Rabbit's briar patch, the old is unthinkable. People cannot stand aging in a society which increasingly reduces the minimal age of acceptance in a social definition of youth. Alvin Toffler, in *Future shock*, speaks of a frustrated nine-year-old who had never been to Europe. Her life seemed meaningless because she felt she had nothing left to experience in the world but a trip to Europe. If a nine-year-old can react this way, should it surprise us that many fathers and mothers regard their children as *youth symbols to be followed and imitated* rather than the other way around? When a man reaches forty, he is at the dangerous age. He may have teenage children; he desires their approval, their affection, most of all, he desires a reaffirmation of his own youth, which is contradictory to the reality of his children.

Many of these men, some of them very distinguished, are faced with long-haired, unwashed, teenage children, trying to organize rock groups, to participate in the new youth culture. Can a man publicly express his feelings about the "new sound" when his children are part of the teenage population creating that sound? Some men can; but some cannot, and these men do society a disservice because they lend a prestige and a respectability to ideas and persons who would never be taken seriously otherwise.

Leonard Bernstein, recognized by everyone as a brilliant, creative man, with an aura of glamor that lends special credence to his opinions in the eyes of some, has endorsed rock. He says it is irresistible. He has written a mass which employs rock idioms. John Green, noted composer-conductor in the film industry, says he does not sympathize with persons who "won't even listen" to the Rolling Stones. John Lindsay, the charismatic idol of youth-oriented politics, leaps upon the stage to applaud the premiere of *Jesus Christ, Superstar*. This is a rock opera intending to portray the life of Christ in new, "mod," "youthful," "rock" terms. All of these men lend their respectability to "rock." There are hundreds of others. They find nothing incongruous in the suggestion that the life of Christ may be portrayed in an idiom which is amoral, and enveloped in a Dionysian subculture of psychedelic hallucinations and psychological rationalization. They find nothing objectionable in the assertion that the soul of American political expression is best exemplified by the public exhibitionism of the late Jim Morrison, who, in the words of writer Joan Didion, "wore black vinyl pants and no underwear and tended to suggest some range of the possible just beyond a suicide pact." They are not frightened or dismayed because Morrison, arrested for indecent exposure, defined the group's interests as "anything about revolt, disorder, chaos about activity that appears to have no meaning."

They are not worried about the prospect that a generation of children, spoon-fed on comic-book culture and spoiled beyond our wildest imaginations, will soon be able to spend part of their daily school hour becoming indoctrinated in the myth that prepackaged "rock" is culture. If these men are concerned, or outraged, or disturbed, they are keeping it to themselves. A distinguished European film composer was summarily dismissed from his Hollywood contract because he was not considered "a viable commercially exploitable writer" despite his shelf of Academy Awards and wide critical acclaim.

Perhaps the most bizarre aspect of all in the rock revolution is the establishment of the vocal and physical freaks as the darlings of the jet set. (Social observers have shifted in their descriptive terms from jet set to Beautiful People to the current "Cat Pack.") Artistic patronage has always been fashionable for the wealthy; Haydn had Prince Metternich, Tschaikowsky had Mme. Meck, and it should not surprise us that patrons of all ages, shapes, and sizes have appeared to exert influence in contemporary music as well. But a hallmark of such activities was always the artistic skill and sophistication of the persons being assisted. The sight of New York's social and literary circles engaged in an almost masochistic pursuit of the non-musicians and non-poets of the counterculture is peculiar. Nik Cohn has commented, "Why pop? Because the yen was all for youth and beauty, and if nothing else, pop was always young, always beautiful. Because pop made its money for itself. Because it spoke so coarse ('Common as dirt, darlings, isn't he divine? '). Because it was what's happening, baby doll. What more reason does anyone need? "

Thus, in what may be the oddest twist of all, the rich, famous and socially prominent turn for a status symbol to lower classes, to the coarseness and vulgarity of a teenage culture gone wrong. The ultimate status symbol, we are told, was to be snubbed by the Beatles or a pouting Mick Jagger, all during the 1960's. In the 1970's, there are new stars ready to accept the plaudits of a worshipful social élite. Occasionaly, however, victims of the rock revolution express themselves in private.

A studio music executive, middle-aged and nervously expecting a purge from his twenty to thirty-year-old superiors, praised the "new sound office." Then, speaking to the author in private, he confided, "They've created a monster, and it's going to destroy us." The word has been handed down. The "do your own thing" rock groups have taken over. They express their brotherhood, their love of humanity, and their self-respect by behaving in the most degrading ways capable of emanating from human imagination. Non-rock musicians need not apply.

Amid this commercial society, which behaves with the spirit of brotherly love found at any medieval court, we hear the critics and academics, afraid of being left behind. Charles Reich, declares deferentially, "It is no criticism of the eighteenth or nineteenth-century geniuses to say that today's music has found a world they never knew." He goes on to describe the over-amplified, ear-deafening montage of writhing, screaming, agonizing rock groups and their mass-mob psychologically captive audience as providing "greater energy than Beethoven's Ninth."

Critics of these middle-aged men, longing for the nostalgia of a young image in the mirror, are dismissed as old fogies. Calvin Jackson proposes that "a Beatle is something you step on — quick." The youth cult, with its conformist dress and conformist, blind adherence to the dictates of *Billboard* and *Cashbox*, insisting that it dislikes labels, dismisses these criticisms. Charles G. Rousculp, a high school teacher and writer, who was Ohio's teacher of the year, counsels, "Adults help the teen businesses along by assuring a constant turnover in teen styles. The cry today is, 'I'd rather be young than be President.' As soon as adults have 'moved in' in their pathetic desire to be teenagers, too, the teenage industries discard the Twist, the Total Look, the 'Yeah—Yeah—Yeah,' or whatever it is, and produce a new teenage something or other. And so the cycle proceeds."

And as the cycle proceeds, the academics and propagandists prepare to draw upon their credentials and their jargon to create a social and ethical basis for the greatest commercial fraud of the twentieth century, possibly in the history of Western civilization.

Rock advocates see the social, cultural, artistic work of the rock groups, and praise their sensitivity, their false morality, their hypocritical life-style, and their imaginary technical competency. There are hundreds ready to follow the false gods of the rock world. Lest we forget, remember the words of Fabulous Fabian, teenage idol of yesteryear, now mature ex-star trying to find a place for himself in a world he is trying to understand: "I was created."

And then recall another Colonel Parker, of another time and place, who said, "A sucker was born every minute, and two to fleece him." Finally, think of Abraham Lincoln, who suggested, "You can fool some of the people all of the time, and all of the people some of the time, but you can't fool all of the people all of the time." Then turn on the radio, the television, the record player, or try "communicating" with your local neighborhood teenager. The youth cult, and its high priests, the rock groups, like the men who designed the Emperor's New Clothes, are ready for you!

III.

THE DRUG MYSTIQUE:
INVITATION TO SUICIDE

The worst sort of hypocrite and liar is the man who lies to himself in order to feel at ease ....Hilaire Belloc

Ignorance is a prolonged infancy, only derived of its charm ....
Stanislaus Jean de Boufflers

If the apologists for the youth culture may be forgiven their ignorance of the fact that rock music is as commercial a commodity as automobiles or toothpaste, they cannot escape so easily when they turn to the drug mystique, a collection of attitudes and ideas that have already been discussed at length in the newspapers and on radio and television. It is embarrassing to argue against the drug mystique; it is equivalent to being asked to explain why earthquakes are unpleasant or why murder should be illegal. But in a day and age when even the obvious may be challenged, it is necessary to do exactly that. The academics and political figures who chastise their contemporaries for not "really listening" to the unwashed creations of *Cashbox* and *Billboard*, are entitled to their taste. If they believe that the soul of American conscience is best expressed by a quartet of feeble-looking males wearing shoulder-length hair, with robust voices worthy of anemic victims of consumption, it is their privilege.

But when they turn to the subject of drugs, they are dealing with a subject which can be analyzed in terms of hard facts and scientific evidence — evidence which condemns them overwhelmingly as men whose desire for the approval of irresponsible youth obliterates what remaining common sense they have.

Within the last several years, a curious aggregation of high-school and college students, professors, politicians, dropouts, and militants, have combined forces in an incredible campaign to proselytize and advertise the drug culture. Drugs have been portrayed as a medium capable of solving all society's problems at once, in terms worthy of a 1910 melodrama. Predictably, the villains of the piece are those scientists or social leaders who regard the use of drugs not as a way to find God or a journey beyond the rainbow, but as a Pandora's box. When thrown open, the box offers a variety of evils capable of dealing death to those foolish enough to believe the propaganda. Pseudo-mature academics and "intellectuals" have been willing to lend the prestige of their social and scholarly positions to a drug culture that can only be deemed suicidal by sane men in search of the truth. Let us examine some facts.

Much of the public's attention has focused upon disagreements over the legalization or decriminalization of marijuana. No longer an isolated problem affecting a single group or age bracket in society, marijuana, or "pot," to use the vernacular, is all over the newspapers. News media have reported instances of students of elementary and junior-high-school age turning to marijuana.

Advocates of pot portray its use as a harmless, spiritual experience with few ill effects. Some persons insist that there is no relationship between marijuana and the use of hard drugs. Others have attempted to persuade us that even such drugs as LSD are a means of pursuing enlightened truth. A large contingent of the academic community is all too eager to sneer and laugh nervously at the insensitive Establishment which conspires to deny progressive adults and their children their truth serum. We may consider the questions of marijuana and other drugs separately, although they are related in many ways. Conclusions should always be based on hard, cold, dispassionate scientific evidence. We turn to the medical and scientific experts for the true facts.

Dr. Edward R. Pinckney, former editor of the *AMA Journal*, told writer Jess Stearn, "It is almost criminal for those so far from the field of medicine or pharmacology to be so dogmatic about something they know nothing about." Stearn has recounted the details of his lengthy investigations into the uses of marijuana and LSD in his book, *The Seekers*. Pinckney referred to a recent medical panel which described marijuana's effects: "postural hypotension (disturbance of normal blood pressure reflexes), mydriasis (excessive dilating of pupils), conjunctival congestion (bloodshot eyes) and frequent photophilia (affinity for light). Muscular incoordination, spasms, urinary frequency, dryness of mouth, nausea, vomiting, and diarrhea sometimes occur. Increase in appetite is common, and has been attributed to hypoglycemia (decrease of blood sugar). Hypothermia (lowered temperatures) has been observed, and some workers have noted a Raynaud-like syndrome (cold extremities and white fingertips). Large amounts of marijuana depress respiration, which is the first sign of impending death in animals given lethal doses." The panel also noted many alarming psychological and social changes. References may be found to panic, gross confusion, implusive and aggressive behavior, depersonalization, depression, and paranoid behavior.

Dr. Luis Souza has presented a report to the Bergen County (N.J.) Narcotic Addiction and Drug Abuse Council suggesting chromosomal damage directly related to the use of marijuana. The American Medical Association has released a report linking marijuana to a psychological dependence capable of producing both emotional and physical ills; included in the physiological dangers were chronic bronchitis, asthma, low blood sugar, sleep disturbance, and impaired coordination.

Dr. Constandinos J. Mitras of the University of Athens, and a Visiting Professor at UCLA, after twenty years of research, has concluded that significant use of marijuana may produce a psychologically lethargic state as a result of or-

ganic brain changes. His tests included evaluation of both
humans and animals who had been exposed to large doses of
marijuana. Dr. Harris Isbell of the University of Kentucky
tested forty humans who used the drug and reported a variety of hallucinatory experiences. Admittedly, scientists
have not completed their investigations into additional physiological dangers and psychological problems that may result
from the use of this drug, but the list of difficulties which
have already been directly related to marijuana is impressive.

Foremost among the difficulties encountered by the user
of marijuana is psychological addiction. When the subject of
drug addiction is raised, pro-drug spokesmen are quick to
assure us that marijuana is non-addictive. Unfortunately,
they do not bother to contend with the psychological effects
of dependence upon marijuana.

Dr. Arthur H. Cain, psychologist and counselor, has out-
lined some of the aspects of psychological dependence upon
marijuana in his highly informative book, *Young People and
Drugs*. He observes that individuals who use pot regularly are
less inclined to work or learn. He goes on to comment,
"This kind of learning simply cannot take place at age
thirty; it must occur during the teens or early twenties. If
marijuana or any drug — inhibitors as they are of curiosity
and learning, of intellectual, emotional, social, and spiritual
growth — becomes even a part-time habit, the individual is
going to reach the age when he should be assuming personal
and social responsibilities in a condition wherein he is quite
incapable of doing so because of his lack of growth in these
essential areas."

Dr. Cain also declares, "I have never known a single
teenager whom I could conscientiously declare sufficiently
responsible for his own behavior, including behavior which
might inflict personal damage, to entrust with even so mild a
drug as marijuana."

In addition to physiological effects, the user of marijuana
may become hilarious or careless; his judgment and memory
may be affected. If his mood is inclined toward depression,
he may become irritable or confused. Dr. Cain suggests that

the mild euphoria of marijuana often serves to ease the guilt that may result from dropping out of society. In any event, dirt or filth are less unpleasant when the person surrounded by squalor is influenced by a drug. Psychologists consider the emotional defense of such drugs by their users to be a sign of addiction.

The report of the President's Commission on Marijuana has confused the issue further. Now, armed with the apparent sanction of a Presidential Commission, apologists for the youth cult are ready to declare pot as wholesome as apple pie. Before they do, they should prepare to deal with the hard questions, the unpleasant realities. These apologists do not choose to acknowledge the fact something is very wrong in a society (or youth sub-culture) which requires regular dependence upon drugs of any kind in order to remain happy or content. The Commission suggested relaxing penalties for private use of marijuana, while continuing to prosecute those who sell pot. Clearly, this is inconsistent. If it is wrong to sell something, it is also wrong to use that product. Opponents of marijuana's legalization saw the Commission's work as an effort to appease advocates of the youth cult, to prove that the Commission was "progressive" and "reasonnable." Advocates of drug use sneered at the Commission for "selling out" to the Establishment by acknowledging, in effect, that the Commission did not really object to private use of marijuana while objecting to public use or sale, at the same time. The President's Commission tried to please everyone, but pleased no one. Some traditionally conservative opponents of drugs have suggested that more time should be spent opposing the dangerous drugs, LSD and various narcotics and stimulants (i.e., amphetamines). But some critics of the Commission have denounced it as producing an unscientific document. Dr. Hardin B. Jones, Professor of Physiology at the University of California at Berkeley, who teaches classes in drug abuse, said that information used by the Commission was worded as if it had been written by potheads. The scientist declared, with reference to his studies of marijuana, that heroin users began their addiction with use of marijuana. He said that servicemen, whose psycho-

logical and behavioral patterns changed drastically as a result
of heroin addiction, turned to the drug after initial experiences with marijuana. Law-enforcement officers were quick
to recognize the legal and moral ambiguities in the commission report. Conservative spokesman, William F. Buckley, Jr.,
urged that marijuana laws be eased, referring to the research
of Professor John Kaplan of Stanford and Professor Lester
Grinspoon of Harvard. Kaplan opposed criminalization and
Grinspoon suggested that marijuana does not harm the individual biologically or psychologically. Los Angeles District
Attorney, Joseph P. Busch, declared, "Medical research into
the habitual use of marijuana is highly inconclusive. Indications of liver damage, vascular brain damage, and ill effects
on the immunity system and healing process — resulting
from long-term use — have not been fully explored." The
District Attorney went on to declare, "Yet [decriminali-
zation] does not take into account the impact of stronger
strains of marijuana, as have been observed in Vietnam, the
powerful extracts of marijuana, and marijuana which is laced
with powerful synthetic drugs such as DMT and TCP."

One is tempted to ask which scientists should we believe? Hardin Jones, Professor of Physiology and Anatomy
at the University of California, Berkeley, suggests that marijuana causes brain damage and that "persons who use marijuana seem to have more deformed babies." Yet we are
assured by a Presidential Commission that these assertions
are less than valid. Perhaps in our efforts to understand
political and social viewpoints from various "experts," we
should keep in mind the observations of former drug addicts,
young men and women who have escaped their former lives.
Gail Bingham, who spent twelve of her twenty-five years as a
drug addict, declared that conservative Republicans "won't
be pushed into legalizing marijuana. They'll stand fast with
the American way, with keeping the laws and not seeing
them ripped out of the books." A twenty-one-year-old
former heroin addict, Ed Mick, said, "We see different politicians trying to legalize marijuana for a few lousy votes. I
don't care what they say about marijuana. It is harmful."
The *Los Angeles Times* reported the establishment of a

foundation for former drug addicts, ninety-five percent of whom favored doubling instead of lessening the penalties for using "pot." All of these former addicts began their drug experiences using marijuana.

Dr. Arthur H. Cain, noted author of books on the drug crisis, counseled young people to think of the future. He said, "Man and woman. These are two things you're never going to be if you remain on pot forever. All you'll ever be is a thirty-year-old baby hippie or a forty-year-old baby hippie, and I doubt very much that you'll live to be much older than that. You're stacking too many cards against a longer life every day you fool around with such chemicals and every moment that you continue to delude yourself that what you're doing is important."

The news media have generally emphasized those aspects of scientific discovery which may be favorable to marijuana. Certainly in recent months, many conservatives have chosen to rethink their own position with regard to pot. Richard C. Cowan, a member of the Young Americans for Freedom, writing in *National Review,* a leading journal of conservative opinion, went so far as to suggest that relaxing of the marijuana laws was an issue that should appeal to conservatives. He insisted that even those of us who take a dim view of the counterculture should revise our stands on marijuana. Cowan's arguments were essentially these: marijuana is non-addictive; it does not lead to the use of heroin; it does not induce criminal behavior, and in moderate effect, does not affect the driving or behavioral habits of persons who have no physical or mental-health problems.

These arguments have become fairly standard, even for those who otherwise oppose the cultural aberrations of the youth cult. But on this particular subject, these usually responsible conservatives seem eager to leap before they look. Dr. Harold Kolansky and Dr. William T. Moore, writing in the *AMA Journal,* reported that all thirty-eight patients who participated in their study of regular pot smoking were adverseley affected. Eight became psychotic, four attempted suicide, thirteen unmarried girls became promiscuous, some with other girls and some with both sexes; of the latter, seven became pregnant. The two psychiatrists also reported that eighteen developed a variety of mental problems, ranging from anxiety and apathy to poor judgment. The remaining patients experienced difficulties in concentrating or remembering, speaking clearly, and distinguishing fact from fantasy. A twenty-four-year old man believed that he was the first member of a new super race; another young man decided that he was a Ku Klux Klan leader who had been placed in charge of the Mafia. The report contained a variety of individual horror stories, often relating the experiences of good students who dropped out of school activities and became disoriented and depressed. Predictably, one of the students, concerned over his depressed mental state, was reassured that marijuana was harmless, by his college counselor. Dr. Kolansky called pot smoking "chemical Russian roulette." Young men and women who were psychotic were able to abandon their delusions after refraining from smoking marijuana, but lapses of memory continued to be a problem.

Even if we accept the suggestion that marijuana would not adversely affect the mind of a man or woman who is totally without frustrations or emotions, such individuals could exist only in textbooks, not in the real world. Even if use of marijuana does not directly lead to the use of heroin or LSD, a society which encourages (or even sanctifies) dependence upon *cannabis* is opening the door for further abuses. As James Burnham, editor of *National Review*, has written, "We do know that frequent use of marijuana is often one element, and chronologically an early element, in the syndrome that includes, chronologically later, the use of hard drugs, though it is also true that in many cases the use of marijuana is not correlated with the later use of hard drugs. Whether pot tends to 'open the door' to hard drugs is an exceedingly difficult scientific problem, but the correlation is frequent enough to bring up legitimate qualm or two to parents watching a child take up pot." As Jeffrey Hart, Professor of English at Dartmouth and author of *The American Dissent*, has wisely observed, the marijuana milieu can lead directly to heroin, even if marijuana itself does not do so directly.

Invariably, discussions about marijuana tend to overlook the positions of governments other than our own. The World Health Organization, composed of one hundred nations who cannot agree about anything else, disagree with the pot smokers. They unanimously voted (including the Middle Eastern nations whose culture has included an emphasis on drugs) to eradicate marijuana by 1985 and to classify it as a dangerous drug. The World Health Organization Expert Committee on Drug Dependence Position on Cannabis (marijuana) declared, "This Committee strongly reaffirms the opinions expressed in previous reports that *cannabis* is a drug of dependence producing public health and social problems, and that its control must be continued. While the marijuana issue has been turned into a holy crusade by many persons who depend on drugs as a means of escape, an even more disturbing element is the acquiescence of parents and teachers. Often, these persons have proven totally unable to recognize the element of peer-group pressure. Let us examine some leading scientific opinions on this subject relating both to marijuana, and the most harmful drugs like LSD. Dr. J. Thomas Ungerleider, founder of Project DARE (Drug Abuse Research and Education), retells the following episode: "I talked to a high-school principal who had forty kids who were stoned in school. He went to the parents. Thirty-six sets of parents told the principal to go to hell. Only four sets of parents came in."

Dr. Mitchell S. Rosenthal, Director of Phoenix House, observes, "There are dangers in the peer group situation. Adolescents are very vulnerable to camaraderie, and the values of the group tend to be infectious. If the group's way of dealing with anger at their parents is to steal cars or use drugs, it is difficult for an individual youngster to resist going along." Rosenthal goes on to advise the parent of a young man who smokes marijuana, "His rationale, that he and his friends and some of their parents see nothing wrong with smoking marijuana, is a very thin veneer. If you don't let yourself be bullied by this pseudo-sociologic bravado, you can get him to think about the real reasons he is using grass. He will discover that it isn't just to feel good or because it is exciting, but because there are things he is worried about, that confuse him. Smoking grass is not going to help that. It will only make him continue to feel like a kid."

If parental irresponsibility is deadly when related to the controversy regarding marijuana, it is deadlier when related to the variety of pills that became fashionable for teenagers of the 1960's, to LSD and the psychedelic drugs, and to heroin. Parents must recognize that peer-group pressure is often very real to the adolescent, and is still a factor on the college campus. Permissiveness regarding family life in general may lead to the assumption that "It's alright to smoke pot." If pot is all right with dad, and mom thinks that junior is just "doing his own thing," it may be all right to try the stronger drugs when they are offered to him.

The difficulty stems from the fact that our society has chosen to make the taking of drugs glamorous and fashionable, and portrays tolerance of drugs as thoroughly chic.

While mature adults will gain nothing by merely expressing outrage at the possibility of their children becoming drug addicts, a greater danger exists. Often, in their enthusiasm to remain "open-minded," they inadvertently encourage the cancerous growth of the drug culture. First, they choose to ignore one of the most important factors in the popularization of marijuana: peer-group pressure. Dr. Fritz Redl, Distinguished Professor of Behavioral Sciences at Wayne State University and a specialist in dealing with the emotional problems of youth, advocates the "peer-group" theory.

He has indicated examples of youthful "friendships" in which true personal relationships are virtually meaningless. Instead, groups of individual young persons gathered, pursuing their own individual fantasy worlds, held together by a peculiar common bond: they avoided their parents and the police, introduced each other to drugs, and encouraged their drug dependence. Often the first samples of hard drugs would be for free, then for a little money. Eventually, when the new friends were "hooked," they would be encouraged to earn their drugs by becoming pushers. The "friends" who persuaded them to adopt this course of action had in turn become pushers through the intervention of their own "friends."

Although Redl counsels against superficial condemnation of youthful drug addicts without an attempt to understand the reasons for their involvement with drugs, he also criticizes the opposite extreme.

He describes the attitudes of some teachers and parents: "Total surrender of clinical responsibility, frequently accompanied by a strange nostalgia for one's own (quite different) youth, or by a freakish over-identification with the young. Not only do the parents of brilliant kids fall into this trap, but I have witnessed highly competent youth-workers and clinicians regress to the incredible foolishness of thinking that the only way of getting rapport with the young is by imitating their hairstyles, their gestures and their dress so as to be considered "in.' "

Redl goes on to recognize some startling reasons for teenage drug addiction. He continues, "For a large number of teenagers, addiction proneness flows from what I would term the handcuffs of the peer-group code. If we piece together the stories told by some of the rehabilitated kids, we learn that their first exposure to hard drugs occurred under the blackmail of this peer-group code. I refer not so much to the specific group of youngsters the kid went around with but to the image he carried of what his contemporaries considered 'a regular guy.' Some youngsters become overdependent on the concept of 'us young people,' usually represented by a fantasized character a few years older, several notches more sophisticated and many degrees less 'respectable' than anyone his parents would admit into their own basement without panic or rage."

Redl applies his criticism not only to parents, but to school administrators, teachers, and guidance counselors as well. In the process of accepting superficial or specious reasons for indulgence in marijuana, these men and women betray their trust and reveal their own lack of common sense.

Michael Aldrich, who divides his time between campaigning for the legalization of marijuana and Yippie politics, offers the hedonistic viewpoint: "Marijuana should be legalized because it's fun." Aldrich's viewpoint, despite its absurdity, is taken seriously by some who should know better.

Dr. Edward Bloomquist, an expert on marijuana, observes that "marijuana is fun" (in his estimation). He suggests that opponents of pot will achieve nothing by refusing to concede this fact. But he wisely goes on to observe that those who follow the Aldrich argument are choosing to ignore the numerous negative aspects of marijuana. Naturally, the fact that some persons consider an activity "fun" is hardly a reason for its legalization. Bloomquist, an articulate critic of the pot-is-fun viewpoint, has the answer. He declares, "One has to place the blame, not on youth who have the right to question and explore, but on those members of the Establishment who have the responsibility of presenting the truth. The tragedy is that some of our older citizens, entrusted with the education of youth, are mature only in chronology. Ideologically and ethically, these people are still adolescent. Through this immaturity, they find their link with youth."

Bloomquist cites the "expert testimony" of Dr. Joel Fort, widely recognized as an "authority" who regards the objections to marijuana as exaggerated. Fort, a sociologist, suggested that pot is unrelated to mental-health problems and not related in a causal way to advancement to hard drugs. Bloomquist, in detailed response, reminds us that his own clinical experience does not support these conclusions. He cites a study by *Psychology Today* which demonstrated a direct increase in tendency to use hard drugs in proportion to the likelihood of dependence upon marijuana. He also cites a bibliography of 1800 articles developed by the United Nations; although advocates of marijuana, lacking his clinical and medical experience, often claim no evidence exists that marijuana can be medically detrimental. Fritz Redl inquires, "Did you ever try to get thirty teenagers enthused about a

Skakespeare drama or a poem by Frost, while half of them are sitting around stoned or asleep? "

The point is well taken. We must beware of "experts" whose little knowledge of marijuana is indeed a dangerous thing.

Some observers believe that America's youth will establish the inevitability of legal sanction for drug activities. Already, high-school students are being urged to think in terms of "declaring their freedom" and "asserting their independence." The direction of this trend may be easily discerned; unfortunately, the path is not the magical road to discovery that some try to present. The Federal Bureau of Narcotics and Dangerous Drugs reports that the number of addicts *under thirteen* reported to authorities has grown thirty-two percent since 1967. This refers only to instances of addiction that have been reported.

Federal authorities speak of pre-teen addiction as being of potentially epidemic proportions. Newspaperman John T. Wheeler reports stories of horror and degradation directly related to the new drug culture. These are not theories or philosophies; they are not manifestations of the Establishment or middle-aged prejudice. They are the cold, hard, realistic facts that exist. The youth cult allegedly prides itself upon "honesty and reality." Apologists for the cult do not choose to be "honest" or "real" about pre-teen addiction. Wheeler discovered a thirteen-year-old Puerto Rican girl who had become a prostitute to keep herself in heroin. At Odyssey House, a New York drug clinic, he encountered a *seven-year-old boy* trying to achieve withdrawal from heroin. A fifteen-year-old Manhattan boy began taking marijuana at the age of ten, then turned to glue. When a friend of his died of a drug overdose, the children attended the funeral, in their own words, "freaked out on heroin." Wheeler related stories of pre-teen addiction from affluent suburbs and wealthy estates to ghettos. Teenage drug-taking occurs in public, on school buses, in full view of friends and neighbors. When advocates of the drug culture talk about the experiences which poor, unenlightened individuals have "missed," they do not choose to include a discussion of the

permissive attitudes toward drugs which ultimately lead
seven-year-old boys to heroin addiction.

Some, as usual, turn to the *non sequitur* argument of
alcohol. (Irresponsibility on the part of young men and
women is justified by the observation that some of their
parents are also irresponsible.) Two basic fallacies exist
whenever the marijuana-alcohol discussion is used as an
excuse to justify the former. First, as Dr. Victor H. Vogel,
parole chief of the California Rehabilitation Center has
observed, marijuana produces distortions in perception of
time and space relations (while maintaining muscular coordination), and a greater degree of tendency toward addiction
and susceptibility. Second, as Alcoholics Anonymous will be
happy to confirm, alcoholism has not been a particularly
desirable element in society. Nine million alcoholics do not
speak well for the argument that marijuana is no more harmful than alcohol. Finally, the California Rehabilitation Center
has released evidence that an overwhelming number of
heroin addicts turned to drugs through the use of marijuana.

Especially in light of the attitude of the President's
Commission, we are told regularly that "young people who
know that marijuana is comparatively harmless, but still illegal will doubt our credibility regarding more dangerous
drugs." This assumption is based totally on the premise that
critical objections to the use of pot are really invalid.

While "progressive" writers and social critics have dwelled
consistently upon the aesthetics of the drug culture, with its
claims of love and brotherhood, they overlook another significant factor: money. The manufacture of drugs with subsequent sale is highly profitable for criminals, who have no
interest in the misery they cause. Dr. Timothy Leary has
been recognized as one of the leading promoters of LSD as a
"truth serum." Leary allegedly attained his popularity because of his charisma, and his ability to communicate with
young people. Yet Glen Carig Lynd, a one-time admirer of
Leary, testified before a California grand jury that Leary's
followers, who organized a "church" called "The Brotherhood of Eternal Love," had been major suppliers of drugs.
Lynd testified that the Brotherhood, which earned thousands

of dollars selling LSD, paid $25,000 to the radical Weathermen organization to help their guru escape from the men's colony in San Luis Obispo. Lynd did not accuse Leary of smuggling drugs, but the activities of the Brotherhood seem clearly to have been oriented toward crime and profit, rather than peace and love. Lynd described drug salesmen who paid $20 a pound for hashish, selling it for $150 to $200 an ounce.

Even a brief look at the facts about LSD shatter the drug mystique, and Timothy Leary's ideas of "revealed truth."

LSD is a drug which, when enough was injected into a 7000-pound bull elephant, caused the elephant to suffer instant death of a laryngeal spasm (loss of muscular control).

LSD is a drug, which, according to Dr. Hans Zellweger, Professor of Pediatrics at the University of Iowa and former Chairman of the Pediatrics Department at the American University at Beirut, is capable of causing congenital birth defects equivalent to those caused by thalidomide.

LSD is a drug which is capable of causing chromosome breaks, which may be inherited by succeeding generations. (In other words, chromosome alterations caused by LSD may be inherited by the grandchildren of the "mod," "enlightened" LSD users. Typical malformations include birth defects involving children who have no arms or legs, legs joined at the hip at odd angles, hands or feet with odd numbers of toes or fingers, and arms or legs in disproportionate size to each other.)

Dr. Howard D. Kurland of Northwestern University and Dr. Charles Yeager of Langley Porter Neuro-Psychiatric Institute of San Francisco reported LSD as the cause of "solid brain damage" after extensive testing of hippies who use LSD.

Dr. Walter Alvarez, formerly of the Mayo Clinic, has observed that sticking together of just three chromosomes can cause mental retardation and bodily defects, and that LSD is capable of inducing multiple misarrangements of chromosomes.

Dr. Edward Pinckney told Jess Stearn, regarding LSD, "It gives many hippies the excuse they apparently require to live the disgusting way they do, since the drugs obviously block out common sense and the proprieties." Pinckney emphasized that drugs were often used to cover the inadequacies of users.

Dr. Doris H. Milmann, a Brooklyn pediatrics professor, had a five-year-old patient who accidentally swallowed a sugar cube saturated with LSD. Within twenty minutes, she became a raving psychotic; nine months later, brainwave tests indicated that her I.Q. had ceased its constant fluctuations. Jess Stearn also reports the case of a professor's wife who shared her husband's expressed interest in LSD. Following experimentation with the drug, she abandoned her husband to seek a romantic interlude with the hippie who had introduced her to the LSD. After the hippie absconded with her remaining financial ressources, following a stay at Haight-Ashbury, she finally became a patient at a San Francisco mental clinic.

In May 1971, a rock group, the Grateful Dead, appeared at a small rock festival (1000 persons is considered small in a field which depends on mob psychology.) An announcement came over the public address system at San Francisco's Winterland Auditorium, advising persons to pass their cold drinks on to their neighbors seated to their left and right. The result? The audience received a mass introduction to LSD. Thirty persons were treated for hallucinatory problems at hospitals.

This was not an isolated instance. A doctor was a regular staff member at the Fillmore East; rock music and drug disasters traveled hand in hand.

The famous exercise of mass indulgence in drugs was clearly the series of rock festivals which appeared to be making a significant impact upon the new youth culture. Names like Woodstock, Altamont, the Isle of Wight, and the "Celebration of Life" festival in Louisiana became household terms. Young men and women by the tens of thousands flocked to these festivals. Reich sings the praises of togetherness, emphasizing rock festivals, an example of what he calls "a community based on having their heads in the same place at the same time."

Was the Woodstock Nation, enveloped in a drug culture, really the Utopian paradise that its supporters would have us believe?

At Atlamon, California, the Rolling Stones were protected by motorcycle gangs armed with chains and knives in order to maintain discipline among the "kids." The promoters of the festival at McCrea, Louisiana, hired a New Orleans motorcycle group which called itself the Galloping Gooses — armed with chains and shotguns to maintain discipline.

Two members of the audience died from drug overdose. First-aid stations were set up to treat hundreds of others who had indulged in what the underground newspapers described as "every known hallucinatory brain popper," ultimately resulting in "bad trips."

In the muddy Louisiana field, members of the audience indulged in mass nude bathing. Reporter Fred Sparks observed, "During the sun-baked days, naked boys and girls frolicked in a nearby river or dozed, sprawled out on rocks like so many lizards." The *New York Times* declared "The sweltering heat made nudity almost essential," compelling William F. Buckley, Jr. to declare this "a finding that would surely raise the eyebrows of some of those who worked in the *New York Times* composing room."

Perhaps the ultimate mockery of the youth cult ideal of brotherhood came at the Goose Lake Rock Festival. Two hundred thousands youths parked their cars in lots named "Layolot," "Astralot," "Tripalot," and "Takealot"; they walked down streets that had been renamed "Kilo Road," "Freak Street," "Zonked Avenue," and "Do It Street" to the entrance. At the gates, each of the 200,000 paid a $15 admission fee; walking past uniformed guards carrying guns or clubs, these peace-loving individuals encountered a mobile unit of motorcyclists, an electrified fence, barbed wire, and a ten-foot brick wall. The security served to keep people inside the 300-acre private park; they came for three days of uninhibited sun, rock concerts, and drugs.

One member of the audience explained his fascination with the drug-rock experience. He confided his feelings to a rock magazine critic. "Like you feel you're in a concentration camp back in Germany," he said, peering through the barbed wire at the armed guards. He concluded, "Like it isn't really America."

Such festivals may be profitable for their promoters, but as collective experiences they may be only interpreted as a form of mututal masochism. The orgiastic mass indulgence in drugs is neither a source for amusement nor a source of pride. It is, rather, a reason to be frightened. Far from the popular image of a celebration of life, this type of activity is a well-policed, commercially exploited exercise in apathetic escapism; it breeds only violence and immorality, and may be politely described as a national disgrace.

Many critics applaud the dependence on drugs of the rock groups; however, they will not choose to comment on the following.

Brian Epstein, thirty-four-year-old creator of the Beatles, died of an overdose of sleeping pills.

Jimi Hendrix strangled on his own vomit after taking sleeping pills and died at the age of twenty-seven.

Janis Joplin died of an overdose of heroin at the age of twenty-seven in Los Angeles.

Brian Jones, at twenty-five, the father of three illegitimate children (three separate mothers) drowned in a swimming pool after taking drugs.

Author Jess Stearn recounted the tale of a girl from the University of California at Berkeley campus who was devoted to marijuana, and promised to write a report praising LSD to challenge Stearn's own anti-drug views. Instead, she was treated at Bellevue after taking pills, slashing her wrists, and putting her head in an oven. Stearn declares, "Of course, it couldn't have been the LSD or pot, for at Berkeley and other institutions of higher learning around the country, they knew these were harmless drugs." Various drugs are offered to the public as a type of truth serum. Unfortunately, when the subject is the drug mystique, advocates of "progressive attitudes" display little concern for the truth.

With the decline of the hippie subculture, many of us have assumed that the drug crisis has ended. Those who do, forget that the basic problem is still very much with us in the 1970's. The dependence upon stimulants is a sad commentary upon the sense of values which pervades our culture. Drugs tend to move in and out of fashion; the drop-out of the 1960's may have dropped back into the mainstream of society, but he may be indulging himself in the ostensibly respectable habits of alcoholism or barbiturates.

The alarming rise of teenage alcoholism is no cause for rejoicing among drug critics. Neither is the campaign to popularize marijuana. Although casual, short-term use of marijuana may not be directly related to drug addiction, we have considerable evidence that long term use of marijuana can cause serious medical difficulties. Can we really believe that the ambiguous medical questions which exist regarding marijuana have been resolved simply because large numbers of people, especially ill-informed young people, have chosen to experiment with it?

The social pressures to indulge in drugs, alcohol, or pills tend to increase. A recent study released by the New School for Social Research incorporated interviews with 426 youthful offenders. 51% of those questioned said they started taking drugs because their friends did it; 19% cited curiosity, while 15% indicated both reasons. None mentioned drug pushers.

In the 1970's, we are faced with enormous temptations. In our tremendous desire to put the generation gap behind us, many otherwise responsible adults have attempted to find out ways of incorporating elements of the youth culture in our own society. In no area does this effort pose a greater threat to a sane and civilized culture than regarding the element of drugs. Allegedly mature individuals must be prepared to recognize elements of hypocrisy which have existed in the past. A parent who lectures his children on the evils of drug abuse in between hangovers can hardly be surprised to find them unsympathetic. But similarly, young people should begin recognizing the need for positive and constructive attitudes regarding the drug crisis. No one has ever successfully refuted the assertion that the greatest reason for dependence of young people upon drugs is social pressure. The mindless need to conform has often triumphed over man's most eloquent logic. The younger generation has no business trying to justify its own indiscretions and excesses by pointing out their parents failures. Two wrongs do not make a right, and two drug or alcoholic habits do not justify each other.

Instead of attempting to rationalize the dependence of large numbers of people on drugs, we should deal with root causes. Instead of trying to make the drug culture more respectable, and using its ostensible popularity as an excuse for pretending it is congruent with a state of normalcy, we must face the facts. People who turn to drugs or alcohol as a means of escape are trying to run away from something, very possibly themselves.

In the case of young people, the stable, contented members of the populace will not need drugs. Those who do, have been unable to resolve important questions in their own lives. These questions may relate to their parents, their fears, or their values. But ultimately, we will have to face the reasons for this dependence. Similarly, those men and women who become alcoholics must not only deal with the result of their habit, but with its cause. This lies at the root of their illness.

One of the greatest dangers to our communities in dealing with the drug question is our concern with fashion. The creation of an exciting and glamorous subculture, riddled with danger and forbidden fruits is a false image for the young to follow. Only by discovering that the forbidden fruits may be rotten to the core can they recognize that we are begging the question. We should not be spending our time arguing about whether one drug or another should be more respectable, more easily accessible, or more popular. Rather, we should concern ourselves with the more basic issue: why do members of our society need to depend on drugs? If it is because our society's values are confused, we should adjust our society. If it is because these people are confused, they must be helped to ultimately help themselves. Either way, we must resolve the causes and recognize the drug culture for what it always has been: an escape from the frying pan, directly into the fire.

IV.

THE TRIUMPH OF SLOBBISM

Bad taste is a species of bad morals . . . . **Christian Nestell Bovee**

As the index tells the contents of the book, and directs to the particular chapter, even so do the outward habit and garments in man or woman give us a taste of the spirit, and point to the internal quality of the soul; and there cannot be more evident and gross manifestation of poor, degenerate, dunghilly blood and breeding, than a rude, unpolished, disorderly and slovenly outside . . . **Philip Massinger**

If any single element creates hostility between members of generations, it is appearance. When conservative Americans are asked what they dislike most about many teenagers or college-age students, almost inevitably someone will mention "long hair" or "far-out clothing" or "beards," or "dirt and filth." But gradually, many middle-aged adults began emulating the customs of these young men and women. Businessmen, afraid to appear old-fashioned, began letting their hair grow. Even a former President was photographed with long hair.

Similarly, fashions starting with the youth cult were rapidly absorbed into the mainstream of society. In the entertainment industry, where images are so important, the older celebrities began to imitate the younger ones. Since the newer actors and musicians were often products of the counterculture, the effect was inevitable. When the new trends in bizarre clothing and appearance were accepted by figures who are glamorized in the press, other middle-aged citizens joined the party. In some respects, the changes in fashion have been exactly that: an elaborate costume ball. But little time has been devoted to the rationale whereby these changes were accepted. If we go back to the origins of all these changes, we find some startling evidence. The new fashions do not limit their influence to clothing alone: they affect taste, manners, and more. They ultimately encourage a new phenomenon: slobbism.

The fashions of the national costume party are well known: jeans, bell-bottoms, shirts decorated in psychedelic colors, tent dresses, etc. Ostensibly, they represent an expression of non-conformity. They are supposed to express the whole person.

As usual, the arguments that support this view are disguised under the label of egalitarianism. Expensive clothing, we are told, enforces social constraints. A rip in a man's suit or a missing button from a lady's jacket are social indiscretions. Therefore, members of the Establishment must constantly be thinking about their clothing for fear of being held in poor taste.

The new clothes, we are told, give the wearer the freedom to do anything he wants. He can read a book, participate in athletic events, gaze at the stars, or even sleep in the same clothes. Everyone is free to be himself, to non-conform, to do as he pleases.

The fallacies in this line of reasoning are obvious. To identify them, let us individually select several neat semantical games played by the advocates of the new fashions. They have designed a clever label with some neat and commercialized packaging: but underneath the wrapper, we find the youth cult, squealing with delight that it's not only all right to look or act like a slob, but it's socially chic and thoroughly intellectual.

The myth of universal function. We are told that clothing favored by the Establishments, suits, dresses, various types of formal attire, are all designed to reinforce role playing. The new clothes are supposed to be functional in nature, functional as all-purpose dress.

It is easy enough to whine about the difficulties entailed in the wearing of suits or dresses, coupled with enthusiastic descriptions of clothes that are equally appropriate for playing touch football or sleeping. But what is clearly missing in this line of reasoning is an awareness that life is essentially composed of disciplines. Life without discipline is not civilized: it is chaos.

This in no way implies that subjugation of one's creative or aesthetic impulses to the commercial dictates of a specific career or specific materialistic values is necessary. "Thou shalt not kill" represents a form of discipline, one to which most men subscribe. The Golden Rule represents a form of discipline. The advocates of slobbism present arguments that are riddled with the inability to distinguish between excessive disciplines (or unfair ones) and those disciplines which *are* necessary. They cannot perceive the difference between a society totally free of discipline and a society in which restrictions are an essential tool in the establishment of true freedom.

The myth of role-playing. Social observers regularly suggest that members of the Establishment wear different clothes for the office, for work, and for play, because they play different roles. Superficially, this may seem to be a discussion of fashion. In reality, it is a consideration of values. Life is made up of responsibilities and pleasures, of triumphs and tragedies, of moments dominated by joy, pain, laughter, and serious deliberation. Life cannot be painted in a single color.

Many young persons who use this justification fail to realize that a man who wears a suit to the office and blue jeans when he plays touch football is merely recognizing that man has many functions in life. They are not the same. The desire for universal sameness is deadly all the more, when one does not recognize its existence. Regular bathing or neat, meticulous forms of dress may be minor inconveniences. Yet the lobbyists for the newest fashions applaud forms of dress, which by their own definitions do not acknowledge that man's clothing (which expresses himself) is not necessarily appropriate for every occasion. If a man is getting married, according to this theory, he does not have to dress more formally at his wedding than he does for a game of touch football. If a woman is giving a concert, she does not have to dress more formally than if she is going camping. Nothing is more important than anything else.

We are all amused by persons who are conscious of purchasing the "best" clothes from the "best" stores. Discovery of a false sense of values is hardly the exclusive property of this generation. A great difference exists between the comical, status-seeking man or woman, who tries to emulate motion-picture stars or figures in society, dressing in poor taste in order to be socially fashionable, and the man or woman who believes that it's dandy to go to church in blue jeans because it's too much work to put on a suit. (We can hear the argument coming: Jesus Christ wore a beard; he preached the spirit of humility.) What these zealots blithely overlook in their attempt to sanctify the unwashed state is that the men and women who gathered to hear the Sermon on the Mount did indeed wear simple clothing; but they did not deliberately cultivate bizarre forms of dress as a means of defying convention or as an expression of a new conformity to the tastes of a group of professional non-conformists. A prime difference exists between the individual who is neat and clean, wearing the best clothing he can afford, and a slob. (Dirt has its place in life; the new arbiters of fashion pretend to dislike sameness, but they do not condemn the universal appeal of dirt.)

Instead we are expected to believe that the right to be filthy in all places is perfectly all right, perfectly apropos in any situation. If a man is going to engage in ditchdigging, certain clothes are appropriate. If he is going to be inaugurated as President of the United States, his dress, his attitude, his manner must be different from his attitude if he is about to dig a ditch. By applying this curious rationale, we may suddenly justify *any* behavior on the grounds that man should not be playing roles.

One need not be serious. Being serious isn't comfortable. One need not dress in a neat or clean manner. This isn't fun. One need not be reverent, diplomatic, rational, or courteous, if one finds these attitudes constraining. Similarly, the clothing that is appropriate for any action is appropriate for every action. We throw our standards out the window. We condemn the pursuit of social status, and embrace the pursuit of comfort. "Comfort," in this frame of reference, means that which is most easily achieved.

The myth of relevance. Slobbism is justified through the excuse of social protest. The slob will respond to criticism of his appearance with the observation, "Do you think poverty or pollution or war is in good taste?" Attention is then shifted away from his self-appointed social critic's inability to govern himself to his ability to govern the rest of the world.

Thus, the pursuit of the radical chic and the fashions of the youth cult lead to a new type of status: irreverence for the Establishment. Although the hippies of the 1960's seem to have disappeared, and the campus ruffians are regrouping on a less vocal level, their forms of dress and attitude toward the social graces is being adopted in American society by the best of families. Thus, it is unfashionable to go to a restaurant or hotel where it is necessary to dress up — this would require a loss of wholeness and self; a dishonest constraint would be placed upon the "now" generation. Significantly, the stores, shops, and restaurants of affluent Beverly Hills, California are filled with young men and women who enjoy the benefits of their parents' wealth while indulging in today's new freedom. Pinning the blame on the Establishment has become easier than pinning the tail on the proverbial donkey. The affluent liberals and their spoiled children can enjoy all the benefits of what money can buy; but by dressing like hobos they can register their anger at the way the Establishment mistreats the poor.

They do not explain why it is appropriate to be unkempt, dirty, or filthy most of the time. Jeans, we are told, express the individual. Bell-bottoms bring dance back into our lives, and they even help us take ourselves less seriously.

Oddly enough, the talk about new forms of dress is devoid of objectivity with regard to the true conformist nature of the youth cult. Frank Zappa, for instance, admits that long hair was a prerequisite for consideration by the record company executives. Society regards Zappa's outrageous appearance as an expression of non-conformity. They do not realize that non-conformity has become fashionable. The real Establishment prides itself on a liberal tolerance for the new mod, hip, where-it's-at variety of nonconformist. In other words, only non-conformists conform to the Establishment picture of contemporary fashion.

If rock music is popular, it is because promoters are selling rock music this season. If bell-bottoms (or psychedelic shirts) are "in," it is because immature persons from seventeen to seventy are trying to keep in step with the journalistic image of youth. *Women's Wear Daily* and *Cashbox* have nothing to do with social relevance.

The myth of social progress. The counterculture has been inclined to hail the conversion of short-haired, neatly dressed young men and women to long-haired, drug-using "freaks." It never mentions filth or dirt; it is difficult to find any sociological justification for dirt, even for those who are adept at leap-frogging important issues. Dirt is unpopular with most people who bathe, and a defense of dirt would undoubtedly prejudice persons who are receptive to the New Politics but still prefer to bathe. No one stops for a moment to consider the almost gargantuan influence of peer-group acceptance in the youth cult. Being accepted by one's peer group has been made an accepted part of social education. Children want to be popular with other children, just as their parents want to be popular with other parents.

Long hair, inevitably uncombed or ungroomed, old jeans, and other all too familiar styles are accepted by the large number of persons who subscribe to the counterculture. Although the hippies are no longer an influence, we have not yet realized that what was called the underground culture of the 1960's has moved into the mainstream of our highschools in the 1970's. The slob may not be found searching for truth in Haight-Ashbury, but he is probably on the local high-school campus. Conformity is conformity, whether to the folkways of Madison Avenue or Haight-Ashbury! Visit your local high-school and college campuses. You will see a large segment of students, dressed absolutely alike. They are being individuals; they are non-conforming.

Young Americans are counseled to "cultivate being outsiders," which may be achieved through clothes, speech mannerisms, illegal activities, etc. One should set out, according to this brand of nonsense, to "non-conform" to a specific set of behavioral patterns, all the while conforming to another set. With this delightful system, a young man can go to school, conform to all the accepted teenage patterns, and simultaneously pat himself on the back because he has escaped the antique social charade of "role-playing." He is misleading no one except himself. The role of "fool" is as old as man himself.

The new youth-culture revolutionaries insist that it is ideal to cultivate the role of an outsider, but execrable to go to the office wearing a business suit because this is status-seeking and role-playing. A double standard is handy for such ideological hopscotch. Youth presumably identifies with minorities and "losers"; Bonnie and Clyde, two notorious bank robbers, were publicized as young people's heroes (banks being part of the Establishment, you recall). Advertising is only objectionable if used to sell products which do not conform to the counterculture. If a Hollywood-New York multibillion dollar film company wants to glamorize "losers," youth understands. A California student newspaper declared defiantly, "Let's tell the Administration that we are going to have a new dress code WHETHER THEY LIKE IT OR NOT! ". This occurred on a high-school campus. At the same school, a girl wrote an editorial in a rage because a school official suggested that the girls be required to dress neatly. Even on the high-school campus, dress codes have the capability· of being used as an excuse for militants' mobilization of. school bodies as tools of the youth cult radical revolution.

The myth of the new taste. Concurrent with the new forms of dress, we witness the demise of taste. In former times, the standards defining "taste" were sharply delineated. Today, however, value judgments vary from social group to social group. Context seems to be of prime importance.

The new taste does not bother with minor distinctions, it simply reverses traditional concepts of taste as a whole. We are fond of smiling at nineteenth-century costumes, at restrictions of behavior, and especially at the chivalrous acts which all men were expected to perform. Taste was regarded as a sense of fitness, of appropriateness. Behavior was influenced strongly by context, and refinement was regarded as a manifestation of society's sense of context.

Edmund Fuller, writing in the *Wall Street Journal*, has described the sudden fascination for "non-upper-class speech" in England, following the rise of the Beatles. Fuller suggests that the reversal of standards, in which lower-class speech and mannerisms are imitated by those above them, is a sign of cultural decay and moral decline. He observes, "Changing tastes in art and manner interact. The effect is not one way but reciprocal. It is commonly argued that art does not influence behavior: Nobody was ever corrupted by a book." But Dostoevsky insisted, correctly, that ideas have consequences.

Edmund Fuller's point is well taken. The artistic manifestations of the new youth culture are often blatantly vulgar and tasteless. He goes on to declare, "The vulgarizing of speech and manners in much current fiction, film, and drama, lends an air of acceptability to the spreading indiscriminate coarsening of talk. It is absurd to suppose that the seeming acceptability of promiscuous sexual bahavior and violence to which these arts expose us does not at least ease the practice of it to some who might otherwise hesitate. This interaction between art and behavior certainly is extensive on the lesser level we call taste and the profounder level we call morals."

Edmund Fuller has thus captured the essence of the youth cult: vulgarity and coarseness. Of course, semanticists try to assure us that all these terms are relative. By doing so, they deny that such a thing as good taste can exist. Rock record companies try to deny that rock music encourages drug use. But the dependence on drugs by the performers, and the saturation of rock lyrics with drug slogans, speaks to the contrary. Apologists for the youth cult assure us that dirty clothing or constant indulgence in profanity are merely expressions of "young honesty." But again, the evidence is to the contrary. If manners, speech patterns, and social behavior lose all sense of context, man's refinement, his degree of polish, the essence of his "civilization" are all gradually eroded. Duncan Williams has gone so far as to suggest that a society whose art, and literature in particular, glorifies depravity, cannot survive at all. In the place of man's refinement, we find what Fuller calls "aesthetic anarchy." We also find a massive effort to persuade us that taste is meaningless.

What we discover instead is a crude, vulgar, uncouth form of man, taking a giant step backward. As "college students, high schools students," and "the kids" learn to discard their upbringing and whatever sense of taste they have been taught, they embark upon a headlong flight toward slobbism.

Perhaps the most curious aspect of the youth culture is the basic assumption of a double standard. If a person is a member of the self-styled "now" generation, he may behave by one moral standard. If he is labeled, the "Establishment," he is expected to behave by another standard.

Any sense of morality is dispensed with entirely. Similarly, the intellectual processes which are used to determine such standards may be abandoned. We may reach conclusions by "knowing" or "feeling" and use these approaches to obliterate a dependence on reason.

"Reason" has had its detractors over the years, not the least of which have been the fundamentalists or ideological conservatives who place great emphasis on "faith." But as always, a distinction exists between faith or feeling and blind irrationality. A man who totally emphasizes cerebral processes may indeed become mechanized, unemotional, and motivated by attitudes that do not take into account human fallibility. But the opposite extreme, the man who reacts violently to society because of feelings or emotions may be in danger of falling into another old cliché: he may be saying, "I've already made up my mind. Stop trying to confuse me with the facts! "

One of the hallmarks of this procedure is the *a priori* assumption that a statement or idea held by self-styled dissenters may be valid by definition, the facts to the contrary notwithstanding.

We assume that some young men and women, because they have recognized the existence of certain flaws in mature society, possess a profound insight into the solutions to those flaws. Similarly, if criticisms are leveled at these proposed solutions, they are to be dismissed and ridiculed as old-fashioned and irrelevant to the contemporary age. Most of us can recognize that an earthquake or a flood is a disaster, but not everyone knows specifically what should be done to prevent these disasters from occurring, or to deal with them after they have occurred. This extends to social problems as well. We have fire departments because every citizen is not thoroughly qualified to put out a fire.

A brief examination of the inconsistencies in some of the statements used to support the assumption of "profound insight" on the part of young men and women who adhere to the drug-rock-bell-bottom syndrome quickly reveals the danger of ignoring facts.

We shall be on our guard for half-truths, conclusions not justified as drawn from premises, *non sequitur*, and enough varieties of inconsistent reasoning to make a tossed salad.

In the new taste, non-conformists are those who refuse to run with the pack. The advocates of the new taste are the conformists; they object to value judgments about their clothing, but do not refrain from using labels (i.e., pigs, Establishment, male chauvinist) to pigeonhole their critics. Their interest in the arts does not extend to the use of speech (or a mastery of the English language). Instead, an inarticulate jargon, a private language, is substituted. Significantly, in the 1960's, the inability of teenagers to express themselves was a teenage phenomenon. In the 1970's, Madison Avenue has taken over, attempting to integrate the new non-speech into the cultural mainstream. Americans are being urged to realize, although they seldom do, that milk has something for every body, and that if you drink milk, you too can become inarticulate.

Raymond Sokolov, writing in the *Saturday Review*, declares, "It's time for the new etiquette." Significantly, the new taste which started in the underground press of the 1960's has started becoming respectable. It is difficult to decide whether to take Sokolov seriously, because the new etiquette is so divorced from etiquette of any kind as to seem almost an exercise in satire. But his attitude, with or without tongue in cheek, is in many ways representative of the new perspectives. He says, "Everyone agrees that morals have changed a lot lately, that virgin brides went out of fashion in the late 1960's, that women are men, although less practiced at smoking cigars, that rags are chic, profanity honest, and old-fashioned good manners a relic of élitist deceit and of sexism from the past." The new principle of the new etiquette is declared to be non-intervention: in effect, the tasteful thing is to let advocates of the youth cult exercise their bad taste in public without being so tasteless as to raise the question of taste. (Parsing that sentence might pose a problem, but then again, "new speak" is here and grammar is part of the Establishment.) The new etiquette, captioned, "Buzz Off, Ms. Post! " speaks for itself. We are instructed not to assume that our unmarried friends of the opposite sex want to share the same bedroom without being so advised, never to expect dress codes, to be as filthy as possible in speech to all women between the ages of eighteen and forty, and wherever possible, to treat women as men.

At the Mad Tea Party, Alice learned about the un-birthday party; it was obviously invented by the youth cult.

In the months since the original onslaught of the dropout culture, conditions have changed for the worse. Many ostensibly mature or sophisticated individuals have found it difficult, if not impossible, to resist the urge to conform. The result has been twofold: there is less of a tendency for the slob to appear strange in a society which emulates his tastes, and our overall decline in matters of grooming has been extending to include a general glorification of boorish behavior.

In the 1960's, we identified people with unkept appearances as "hippies". Today the differences are considerably less distinct. But the major difficulty in dealing with slobbism remains. We persist in seeing the question of taste and style as simplistic arguments over dress codes, thus disregarding the overall cultural implications of such trends. It is not surprising to find large numbers of adolescents who are, to varying degrees, unkempt, ill-mannered, and inarticulate. Richard Armour, in his book "*Through Darkest Adolescence*", suggested that the teenage years could be easily understood if we regard them as a childhood disease like the measles.

What *is* surprising and unique regarding this particular generation has been the way in which the normal adolescent behavior has been treated by the parental generation. Instead of dismissing teenage fads and mannerisms, a good many otherwise sensible adults have accepted them as youth symbols, to be cultivated and emulated.

It is this deliberate cultivation of bad taste and uncouth behavior which is frightening in its implications. In every instance of strange or anti-social activity, we tend to find a conscious effort to foster our worst instincts. Ugliness has been proposed as an ideal. Apologists for this new standard have suggested that a glorification of ugliness is a means of achieving a new tolerance. Not every woman is beautiful; not each man is handsome. Particularly during the self-conscious teenage years, it is only natural to seek some sense of reassurance regarding one's physical appearance. If society no longer places an emphasis on skin-deep beauty, it could be all to the good. The tendencies toward dirty, unkempt appearances, or a minimum of clothing emphasizing nudity, is infinitely more derivative of teenage rebellion than profound insight into the nature of inner beauty. The adolescent who cultivates the most outrageous hair or dress styles may be vulnerable to charges of gross exhibitionism, especially if his prime motivation is to satisfy his peers that he, too, is willing to conform to their standards.

Nor is this tendency to glorify the ugly appalling only to those who are conservative, stuffy, or backward. The image of the non-conformist as a "swinger", a free-wheeling adventurer who keeps up with the times, is absurd. The true nature of such conformity disguised as dissent is recognized by many astute observers of our social and cultural decline. Anita Loos, whose renowned best-selling book, "*Gentlemen Prefer Blondes*", chronicled the escapades of the 1920's, and the generation of young people to whom this one is often compared, is a case in point. She observed, "It is only normal for grownups to want to look young, with the result that, in copying the teen-ager, they, too have embraced its cult of ugliness; ladies of erstwhile dignity uncover knees that are bulgy from years of too little exercise; women with well preserved bodies assume the sleaziness of bell-bottom pants, which give them the proportions of Popeye the Sailor Man. And dress designers in Paris, London, New York, and particularly Hollywood, have followed along with the trend."

She goes on to suggest that a modern-day "Cinderella" could be produced in Hollywood with the characters reversed. Cinderella would be an ugly girl, forced to bathe and wear beautiful clothes, until liberated by a fairy godmother who provides her with a fright wig and arranges for her to meet Prince Charming, a cigar-smoking hippie who cultivates his drug habit in the East Village.

Admittedly, not every motion picture need be devoted to the exploits of stars who are as attractive as Cary Grant or Grace Kelly. But in the 1950's, glamour was regarded as an ideal to be achieved. Those who were not instantly handsome or beautiful could still admire or emulate the style and sophistication of screen images. Today, as Anita Loos has astutely observed, writers and producers have followed the visual arts in emphasizing that which is vulgar or unappealing. It should surprise no one that the emphasis on ugliness encourages young people to deliberately cultivate their worst features. Joan Crawford once said she would not dream of stepping outside her door without looking the way people expected a star to look. Today's film and television stars talk about a lack of vanity, but their obligatory uniform of faded denims or pathetic attempts to appear *au naturel* are more indicative of slovenliness than humility.

The President of a major university in Southern California once remarked that his son purchased a new pair of jeans and then deliberately set to work fading them for weeks. The trend toward patchwork clothing has struck some fashion conscious individuals as amusing. They do not realize that a society which regards anyone who is neat or clean as "square" is turning its values upsidedown.

Similarly, the inability of young people to express themselves is being absorbed into the mainstream of society. Edwin Newman, in his book, "*Strictly Speaking*", suggests that a modern-day Shakespeare would present Hamlet inquiring as to the meaning of life in these words: To be or not to be, y'know . . . like, that is the question.

Adults who wonder why young people seem unable to express themselves in a literate, articulate fashion should look no further than the public school system. Teachers, convinced that they must communicate with the children at their own level, have increasingly abandoned an emphasis on English fundamentals. Since children do not like to read, the teachers blithely assume that *anything* a child reads is good for him, simply because he is reading. So these self-styled pedagogues, deciding that they cannot expect children to read anything but what interests them, hasten the demise of good reading from the beginning. Dividing his time between a steady diet of television and an assortment of comic book level publications provided at school, junior proceeds to grow. By the time he is a teenager, junior vocabulary tends to be influenced by the people around him: his peers, whose assorted "likes" and "y'knows" prevent them from achieving coherency, his teachers, who are afraid of discouraging him by demanding a level of concentration, and his parents, who are worried about being accused of being old-fashioned.

The result is a mentality which cultivates an ugly, unkempt physical appearance, and is exposed only to the crudest forms of verbal expression. Playrights and novelists have been quick to jump on the bandwagon of incoherent expression. The assumption that poetry or prose must be taken seriously simply because they exist is ridiculous. Yet today's young people can, with full support of the schools, grow up without any recognition or awareness of music, books, theater, or art, which is not specifically a part of the teenage subculture already. The result is that the typical teenager falls prey to an old creative trap; he likes what he knows. Since he doesn't know very much, because no one has ever demanded that he expose his mind or his tastes to anything else, his horizons are limited.

The basic fault, of course, lies not with young people, who don't know any better, but with adults, who should. Junior looks around and sees an odd assortment of figures who are the heroes of his peers. Since the teenage heroes are invariably unkempt, slovenly individuals who mumble their way through the English language, why are we surprised to find the obvious result? Young people from the best homes and families consciously work to make themselves ugly and dirty, and to emulate the speech habits and lifestyles of those who give them the least thought. It requires very little work to look like an unmade bed. Casual neglect thus becomes the hallmark of the young. As the more extreme teenagers try to appear nonchalant they allow themselves to appear in public looking progressively more outrageous. The middle-aged adults of the copycat variety regard such slobbism as a form of sophistication. The dash and glamour of former times have been replaced by a new ideal in which man's most primitive instincts are also regarded as his most desirable.

The Metropolitan Museum of Art, in New York, presented an exhibition of Hollywood costumes, dating back to the 1930's. Many of those attending the exhibition were astounded to see young people, gaping open-mouthed at the dress styles of 30 to 40 years ago. A generation raised on faded jeans and uncombed hair can only be surprised by an approach to grooming they have never seen. Similar reactions have been reported regarding the responses of young people to their initial encounters with Shakespeare, jazz, or any of the art forms which have been exiled to oblivion during the last decade, in deference to teenagers.

As the natural tendencies of teenagers are encouraged, we find ourselves with a new dilemma. The rebellious youth, surrounded by peers who have already discarded most of society's standards, seeks new ways in which to shock his elders. With speech and dress styles already cast aside, he must find more outrageous ways of distinguishing himself from the normal side-show of inarticulate teenagers who are now regarded as American as apple pie. He does not have to look very far for models.

The rise of the cult of the anti-hero has been chronicled and dissected. As our tastes and standards have become increasingly jaded, it has become necessary for those who seek to shock society to become more and more extreme. Today, the man who speaks of bad taste will be ridiculed. We have been conditioned by a pretentious pseudo-sophistication to accept bad taste and vulgarity as a norm. The idea of being "with it" or "hip" has become irresistible to a good many citizens who never stop to ask themselves precisely what or whom they are so eager to be with.

In recent months, we have witnessed a variety of new idols who have been paraded before the public as examples of new or revolutionary experiments in taste. Concurrently, we are subjected to a host of revivals and rediscoveries regarding figures whose overt vulgarity or obscenity was once considered offensive. These individuals are now being re-evaluated by a permissive society, eager to recant its puritanical past and to do penance, as only a community of swingers can, for being less than receptive to bad taste.

The classic example of such re-evaluation is Lenny Bruce. Through a variety of commercial exploitation schemes, the comedian has been made the central theme of a major play and subsequent film. Biographers inform us that "Lenny's time has come". Once ostracized for his dependance upon obscene language, Lenny Bruce has achieved through a dubious legacy what he failed to achieve during his lifetime: a hero-worshipping cult which regarded his obscene tantrums as social satire. Bruce's tour of Australia was typical of his escapades. He talked about a variety of subjects during his nightclub routines: various kinds of sexual relations, what one newspaper called a blasphemous account of the crucifixion, and peppered his speech with a variety of obscenities.

When his performance caused the expected storm of controversy, he retired to his hotel room for a diet of ice cream and heroin. Today his suggestion that "obscenity is in the ear of the beholder" is regarded as profound. We fail to recognize it as simplistic nonsense.

Bruce died naked, on a toilet, attempting to inject a drug into his arm. He is a poor excuse for a legend, and his principal claim to fame was a foul mouth. Yet today, there is a popular assumption that obscenity is truth and that a steady stream of vulgarity has meaning. A four-letter word vocabulary is easy to acquire; the assumption that obscenity is all a part of the imagination rejects the equally important standards of morality and taste at opposite poles. If we assume that the use of obscene language in public lessens the pungency of such speech, we would do well to remind ourselves that profanity is primitive, and to limit ourselves (or our artistic expression) to such levels denies the expressive quality of our language or the reality of man's highest emotions. The usual excuse we are offered is that standards of taste and morality are old-fashioned, and that only through a blood-and-guts indulgence in the language of the gutter can we express reality. The novelist and poet Robert Nathan observed that both a sewer amd an April meadow are "real". It is entirely up to us upon which thoughts we choose to concentrate.

The glorification of all that is ugly in society is in part a manifestation of the ways in which commercial interests choose to exploit man's basest instincts. If teenage girls go to school looking as if they are dressed to offend the vice squad, why should we be surprised if they act accordingly? If teenage boys idolize the misfits of society whose only achievement has been rebellion for its own sake, what do we expect them to do? If parents and teachers regard the advent of slobbism as cute, funny, chic, sophisticated, or a manifestation of non-conformity, can we fail to be offended by their lack of perception?

The debate over slobbism is not a simple question of dress codes or good English. It strikes at the very heart of the matter. The essence of a civilization is to be civilized.

The challenge is ours. A plethora of false idols can lead to man's cultural decline. We tend to concentrate so militantly on potential political or military decay, that we forget our cultural perspective. A society of ignorant, uncouth, unkempt boors, is hardly worth saving. It is our duty and responsibility to see that the trends which clearly herald the advent of such a society are reversed.

We are told that man's imperfections must be tolerated. There is a distinct difference between tolerance and encouragement. As Anita Loos wrote recently, "Let youth damn our hypocrisy as it may. I have never been able to condemn it. It has always seemed to me a sort of good manners of the spirit. We are assured by the Bible that nobody is perfect; but when we put on the outer trappings of perfection and try to ape a certain purity of heart, it shows that we are not in agreement with our imperfections. In other words, we try."

Our society will not necessarily prosper because boys try to be handsome or girls beautiful. The rituals of courtesy may not guarantee honesty in politics. Man's moral essence is not governed by a crew cut. But neither should we accept the pompous and supercillious assertions that slobbism is justified as a protest against hypocrisy. The foul-mouthed ignoramus tries to rationalize his behavior by talking about artificial, plastic values of society. He fails to realize that his own values are more artificial than those he criticizes. If the counterculture of the 1960's had a message, it could have delivered its message through a literate medium of communication. Those of us who criticize slobbism are often accused of emphasizing the style and tone of the counterculture rather than its content. But the content, the lifestyle, the essential message of the dropout society *were* its communication.

Our politicians should be both clean *and* honest; the absence of the rituals of courtesy of dress or demeanor will not help society. If our film stars or public idols are people of taste, style, and quality, we are encouraged to cultivate our best rather than worst instincts. The type of society we foster as mature adults is indicative of the society in which young people are raised. So the ultimate responsibility falls square where it belongs: upon our shoulders. By aspiring, by trying to achieve man's best, we may in part succeed. By contriving to accept our imperfections, and deliberately fostering the neglect of our standards, we shall surely fail.

V.

WHAT THE KIDS WANT

Youth, when thought is speech and speech is truth   Sir Walter Scott

Youthful rashness skips like a hare over the meshes of good counsel
. . . . . William Shakespeare

The English language is constantly changing. New expressions arise every day. Yesterday's fashionable expressions are suddenly laughable clichés today, and today's relevance becomes tomorrow's memory. But one expression that is becoming a deplorable constant in the contemporary vocabulary is "the kids" or invariably, "what the kids want." Not the children. Not the young adults. Not the young men and women — the kids.

In the heated discussions that erupt whenever adults converse on the whys and wherefores of young men and women, very few people bother to explain exactly who or what they consider "the kids" to be. Yet the media are constantly reporting public statements by eminent figures relating to "understanding what the kids want." Many persons assume that all "the kids" want the same things, or that certain self-proclaimed spokesmen are entitled to speak for the younger generation as a whole. Occasionally, a middle-aged adult professing to "understand the kids" will try to emulate those members of the younger generation of whom he approves.

Amid the confusion, it is necessary to remind ourselves of some basic facts about the younger generation. We must stop indulging in clichés about "the kids" or "what the kids want," and try to determine who, if any, are the true spokesmen for the younger generation.

Being "old" or "young" is relative; any adult may seem "old" to a small child, and even grandparents may seem "young" to a man who has attained his hundreth birthday. When mature adults speak about "the kids," many are not entirely sure which age group they are discussing. For example, when a recording company executive talks about "the kids," he may be discussing the nine-to-fourteen-year-old audience whose preferences dictate the stylistic direction of the multibillion dollar pop-music industry. When a university president refers to "the kids," he may be talking about post-adolescents or teenagers about to enter college. When a politician criticizes "the kids," he is undoubtedly thinking of political militants. Yet many of the self-proclaimed leaders of certain groups of political militants are curiously over thirty. By definition, one cannot expect the same tastes, desires, behavior, or social outlook from a nine-year-old who wants to buy the latest Beatle record and a thirty-five-year-old professional political militant who travels around the country trying to incite violent revolution. Many young persons fall chronologically between these two extremes. Most important of all, large numbers of young men and women do not adopt the attitudes or characteristics generally attributed to "the kids." These young men and women are often ignored because they do not conform to a preconceived notion of the younger generation developed by persons of middle-age.

Therefore, if any intelligent conclusions are to be drawn regarding the younger generation, it is necessary to first distinguish between various age groups in that generation, and to recognize the existence of individuals within those age groups. The younger generation can no more be divided into a neat group of categories than the older generation.

Because parents are responsible, to a great extent, for the perspectives their children develop, it is also advisable to take a long, hard look at the institution of parenthood today; we must try to determine why parents and children behave the way they do at this particular point in time.

Differences exist between juveniles, adolescents, and young adults. In considering the relationships between parents and children, we must remember the distinctions in behavior of juveniles, and their older counterparts who "drop out" of society, and those political activists who wish to control society while characterizing themselves as dropouts.

So much attention has been devoted to members of the younger generation that their parents have been neglected. The parents of the current generation provide the key that explains many of the dilemmas facing society today.

The current generation of teenagers was born in the 1950's. College students in their twenties were born after World War II. Their parents were in college (or in the armed services) during the late 1930's, 1940's, and 1950's.

Vivid memories of the depression affected many of these parents. Material security was of prime importance to men and women who had experienced varying aspects of the economic catastrophes of the 1930's, the recovery traumas of the 1940's, and the horrors of war. Simultaneously, parents desired to provide a better life for their children than the life they had experienced. Children growing up during the 1950's were not faced with wars or financial catastrophes. Americans recall the 1950's with nostalgia because these years seemed relatively free from trouble.

Of course, the post-war period was not free from problems; many of our present difficulties may be directly traced to conditions that existed during that period. Parents, trying to practice an "enlightened" attitude toward their children, depended heavily on progressive education and child psychology with regard to attitudes on discipline, authority, goals, and values. Ironically, the new economic boom of the 1950's encouraged these new attitudes. The children of the 1950's (gradually growing into the young rebels of the 1960's and the young men and women of the 1970's) were exposed, for the most part, to great prosperity. (The youth cult approaches the American economy as if it were composed of tycoons and manual laborers, with no socioeconomic groups in between.)

Parents were eager to let their children enjoy the freedom from cares that suddenly seemed to be available as the war ended and depression memories receded. They were also intent on pursuing a variety of materialistic goals themselves to provide greater security and greater financial rewards.

In short, parents were enthusiastic in their pursuit of a world that would be totally opposite of the world they knew as children: a society dominated by depression and war.

Combining a desire for financial security with a variety of new psychological fads, parents became permissive as never before. Domald Barr, Headmaster of the Dalton School and author of *Who Pushed Humpty Dumpty?*, has commented, "We offer very little resistance to our children. We tend to withhold reality from them by behaving as if there were no such notion as earning things ... we think unthinkingly (so to speak) that 'yes' is a loving word and 'no' is a hostile word ... Indulgence sometimes is, and is usually taken for a lack of concern; better the father who roars than the father who shrugs."

Barr's point is well-taken. Parents were often busily pursuing their own financial security. (They were also seeking security for their children. But they saw this security in material terms.) Providing a "good life" meant a secure life; material security was stressed as an alternative to close family ties. These family obligations became less important, because father and mother were busy with other obligations.

Thus, parents, reluctant to accept parental responsibilities, maintained a pretense of family life while disregarding its basic tenets. The results were predicatably disastrous.

As parents confused love and affection with financial security, they also failed to distinguish between "love" and "permissiveness." This permissive attitude was aided and abetted by the emergence of a new "emancipated woman." Mother was not home when junior returned from school; she was pursuing a variety of careers or pleasures. Junior, of course, was enjoying a better life than his father had. When father was a small boy, he might have found his mother waiting at home for him when his school day ended. He might have faced some youthful responsibilities, because in the depression or post-depression years, a paper route or a summer job might have been essential as a means of helping the family. But such minor matters are of little concern to junior, since both 1950's parents were probably working.

The parents, of course, were blissfully ignorant of their folly. They were "giving" junior what he needed: anything his heart desired (in a material sense). Many parents justified their lack of real interest in their children by satisfying these material whims. From their standpoint, junior has "everything"; from his, he had a relationship with two persons who fell somewhere in between Santa Claus and the proverbial gift horse.

Many parents were hypocrites. Parents verbally stressed certain moral and social codes. Often, they advised, in effect, "Do as I say, not as I do." Father might insist that junior "Always tell the truth." But his father spends time boasting about his success cheating on his income tax, junior does not receive an emulative example.

Similarly, mother advised daughter about a strict and traditional moral code, especially with reference to marriage. But if mother indulged in a promiscuous affair with her husband's boss, daughter's adherence to a strict moral code regarding a premarital affair of her own should surprise no one.

Today, many parents are outraged if junior sneers at marriage, yet they themselves are often practitioners of infidelity. As a result, any teenager who knows how to spell "p-i-l-l" and thinks he or she has discovered some biological truths unknown to the rest of society may embark on a promiscuous life-style at a moment's notice. The old, outdated moral codes of the 1950's become sources of amusement for the sly jokes among the pseudo-sophisticates of the 1970's. "Free love is nothing new," a confident teenager will declare today. "Our parents did the same thing, but they didn't talk about it. But we're different. We're honest. We tell it like it is."

Advocates of the "new morality" subscribe to this attitude, offering as an excuse the cliché that the young are suspicious of contracts, i.e., responsibilities that have been recorded. The point that advocates of the "new morality" miss totally is that in the promiscuous 1950's, mother and father were not adhering to the moral code they preached. This does not invalidate their moral code, which they chose to ignore. If many "mature" adult Americans have failed in marital relationships, the fact, in itself, does not justify the dismissal of marriage as an institution. Similarly, parents who pontificate about "honesty" while practicing "dishonesty" have not discredited the ideal of honesty; they have only emphasized the importance of an ideal to which they have failed to adhere, just as their children have failed. Junior cannot justify his behavior by saying that his parents are "wrong" about something. Possibly, both are wrong!

The basic principle is applicable in a variety of circumstances. If father tries to tell his son about the dangers of drugs, he will undoubtedly be reminded about any difficulties he has with alcohol. An alcoholic father does not represent justification for junior's becoming a drug addict. A promiscuous mother does not serve as an excuse for daughter to sneer at the institution of marriage. She may justifiably sneer at her mother's interpretation of marital fidelity. There is a difference.

Apologists for the youth cult are eager to beg the question. Whether or not father loses his equilibrium after the fifth martini has nothing to do with the medical facts about marijuana; such an assertion is irrelevant to the sensibility of drug addiction.

The father who does not overindulge himself can try to persuade junior to behave in a intelligent manner without negating his own advice through his own actions. Parents go to church and mouth the concepts of their religions: but do they practice what they preach?

An essential error in the thinking of apologists for the youth cult is the inability to distinguish between the failure of institutions and the failure of men to observe those institutions.

Parents seldom prepared children for the vicissitudes of life. Television represented a medium in which problems were finite and could be solved in thirty-minute or one-hour segments, with generous time for commercial advertisements. Children became accustomed to instantaneous solutions. In the real world, such solutions are not to be found. Young people find it difficult to reconcile the rules of behavior that they were expected to uphold as children with the realities of the adult world. Adults may choose to respond by observing that right and wrong are intrinsic values which are not negated by the confusion of the real world. This argument is only valid if the parents themselves adhere to the ideas of "right" and "wrong" they propose. If parents cannot live by the standards they impose on others, they fail as parents. Men and women who prepare their children to live in a world seen through rose-colored glasses have not prepared them at all.

Eventually, junior has a rude awakening. The children of the 1950's had their rude awakening when they found out that idealism is not easy in a world which regards profit, not principles, as a pragmatic solution to philosophical questions.

The dangers of instantaneous gratification and solutions may be seen in the manifestations of violence relating to youthful political activism. If junior wants something changed, he wants it changed now! He may not be interested in the way these changes may affect others. Problems facing society today are highly complex; they cannot be solved or eliminated through meaningless clichés or political slogans. Junior, of course, is accustomed to having matters handled his way, because at home his material needs have been gratified instantly. Unfortunately, society is full of persons who desire to maintain the status quo, and equally full of those who want to dispense with the status quo instantly, but have no idea what to offer in substitution. If changes are not made instantly, junior will throw a tantrum. Thus, a college is presented with a series of non-negotiable demands. (The demands junior makes at home are never negotiated; father and mother give him what he wants.) The demands may be immature, irrational, silly, or even impossible. But they must be gratified. If not, junior may be encouraged by outsiders (who are promoting their own interests,) to burn down the Student Union if the administration will reject the non-negotiable demands. (This is highly unlikely; university presidents are usually eager to agree to demands, because implicit in their agreement is the understanding that they are reasonable, rational men who believe, like the indulgent 1950's parents, that "Yes" and "No" are synonymous with love and hostility, respectively.)

Parents are surprised that junior is insistent on having his way — his instant solution to the ills of the world. Why? They have always gratified his whims. Can they legitimately blame him for being surprised that the rest of the world fails to do likewise?

Parents became followers, not leaders. A parent can hardly expect respect from a child if the *raison d'être* of his existence is the demonstration, through speech patterns, dress, and general life-style, that he has not lost his long vanished youth.

In their desire to be open-minded, parents are permissive. Most children possess an atavistic tendency toward mischief. But parents, eager to prove that they are not ogres, tossed discipline out the window. If five-year-old Johnny or six-year-old Mary breaks other children's toys or destroys property in school, we are told "Johnny and Mary are expressing themselves." When the children grow up and go to school, they will encounter professors who applaud their new disrespect for private property. The professors aren't telling the youngsters something they haven't known all along. The assertion the "people matter more than property" is a sterile cliché when used as an excuse for one man to take what belongs to someone else. Society possesses an overabundance of persons who want what someone else has. If every man fosters disrespect for another's property, he can have no complaint when someone desires to appropriate his property using the same rationale.

In later years, of course, if Johnny or Mary demonstrate a proclivity for irresponsible or criminal behavior, parents, quick to excuse themselves, wonder who is to blame. Johnny may have been an incipient menace to society as a child; Mary may have required some strong discipline at an early age. A parent who is afraid to teach his child respect, while filling his life with material comfort, is raising a spoiled malcontent; he should not be surprised that when junior decides to tell society where to go, he will include his parents in the invitation.

The juveniles who adopt the fashionable hairstyles, costumes, and speech patterns of their friends are not really indulging in profound social protest, any more than Huckleberry Finn was expressing sociological subtleties when he said "ain't." Children often adopt the patterns of speech around them, basic to their environment. If a child is not guided into a conscious observance of the precise function of words, he may become verbally inarticulate. (Is a long-haired, slovenly, eleven-year-old boy who says, "I'm what's happening," or "I'm where it's at! " expressing complex emotions? Hardly. He is merely conforming to the fads and fashions of his peers.)

Today's affluent neighborhoods may claim a plethora of boys and girls who emulate their thoroughly modern elders, the long haired, unwashed post-adolescents. Incredible as it may seem, certain self-styled mature adults are determined, at all costs, to regard these overindulged youngsters as polemicists for a new youth culture that must be emulated. (Most pre-teen children are inarticulate or grammatically careless because they don't study their English lessons carefully.) If these juveniles live at home, supported by their parents, attend school, and adopt only the superficial physical trappings of "hippies" or "now" generation college students, they are immature conformists; nothing more.

This same principle applies to high school students who adopt these mannerisms. The process of social isolation which is generally described in the press as "dropping out" refers specifically to those young men and women who leave home and seek a new life-style. (The validity of this life-style may be surmised from previous statements relating to drugs, rock music, and the deliberate cultivation of slobbism as a panacea for personal inadequacy.)

The first step in achieving a mature, intelligent perspective regarding the state of affairs on campus is the recognition that the academy may not quickly be divided into a neat, facile set of classified "heroes" and "villains." Many legitimate grievances *do* exist regarding the way universities are managed. As society placed greater and greater emphasis on a college degree, the value of that degree declined. The cycle continued to run its course with the subsequent devaluation of Master's and Ph.D. degrees. More and more students appeared in graduate school; as these advanced degrees became more ordinary, and holders of such credentials more numerous, tremendous pressures were placed on both students and faculty. The result of an environment on campus which encouraged the existence of institutions which were overpopulated with persons who really didn't belong in college at all, was a great expansion.

It is difficult to determine any sense of logical or sensible growth on the part of academic institutions. Many of these schools are huge: massive, towering edifices, housing dozens of classrooms, crowded with persons of every size, shape, background, and with varying degrees of intelligence.

Much of the time a student spends in a university is devoted to procedures and processes which have little or nothing to do with education. A student is expected to assign many valuable hours to filling out reams of forms, paying heed to numerous pontifical procedures of protocol which do not make sense to anyone.

The university employees who receive the least amount of attention, an odd assortment of secretaries, teaching assistants, registrars, credit evaluators, and other persons whose precise functions remain a mystery to all, even themselves, cannot be ignored. (Lawrence Peter, educator, humorist, and creator of the "Peter Principle," calls them "professional automatons.") Often these people foster an obsessive concern for the keeping of records, the maintenance of files, and the evaluation of individual achievement against a cookie-cutter model which is capricious and arbitrary. University hirelings are prone to deferring to "the catalogue" or "the rules," although they are often unable to explain why there is any justification for these rules.

This attitude extends into the classroom. Ostensibly students attend a university for purposes of receiving an education. (Students often attend for other reasons. Husband hunting and political opportunism are as respectable as ever.) But many of the traditional means of evaluating a student's capabilities are anachronistic. The pupil is constantly tested or examined; the tests and examinations are usually less related to a student's ability to think or reason than to his capacity to participate in a social *pas de deux* with his instructors.

In large universities, the teacher may be a graduate student or teaching assistant, frustrated because the senior professors have free time to pursue their research or independent careers, while he must teach. In a typical general studies lecture course, the student may sit in a large classroom of fifty or a hundred young men and women, listening to a professor lecture for an hour. The teacher himself may be dull, disinterested, or bored. He may choose to read his lecture notes in a monotone, droning away while his charges glance wishfully at the clock, hoping that something exciting will occur to put them out of their misery. (This condition is not new; what makes it especially serious at present is that it continues to get worse, not improve.)

The student is expected to take notes during the lectures, and then memorize these notes, along with a lengthy textbook. Then the student attends his examinations, and is graded primarily on his capacity to parrot the lecture notes or facts extracted from the textbook. The professor may not possess the slightest inclination to discuss, to argue, or to inquire, all activities which are eminently respectable in the academic tradition. If the professor chooses a multiple-choice test, the grade may be assigned by a teaching assistant, or by a computer which corrects the student's papers. When this procedure is carried to its ultimate extreme, the professor is photographed reading his lecture notes while the students sit in another room watching their teacher on closed-circuit television.

The student may be expected to devote much of his time to courses or requirements which may have utterly nothing to do with his chosen career. If the student has not chosen a career, he may be using the classes in an effort to find himself; many young men and women are unsure of their goals or perspectives. They may need time and experience to reflect the ideas, goals, and values which may determine their future destinies. If a young man or woman comes to a university under the illusion that he will be encouraged to think, to analyze, to contribute, and to participate in a meaningful way, he is often exposed to a bitter disappointment. The elimination of outmoded procedures in the academy in no way implies a fostering of mediocrity or a debunking of excellence.

But if the student is expected to participate in an academic community which functions according to false values, not "knowledge" or "education" or "intellectual pursuit of excellence," but forms, catalogues, overcrowded classes, and arbitrary sets of rules, all of which serve to isolate the student in impersonal and dehumanizing ways, the student often responds in kind. (Emphasis must be placed on the word "arbitrary" when existing rules are criticized. Too often otherwise intelligent persons will imply that all "standards" or "rules" must be abandoned.)

If students knew more than their teachers (about specific subjects), they would have no business being students. A pupil does not instinctively know what curriculum is best for him; often we are exposed to ideas which may seem useless at the time, but valuable later in life. What is severely lacking in the colleges and universities is a capacity to slow down the machinery of the campus long enough to evaluate college procedures in a sane and sensible way.

Many firms make small fortunes selling pirated term papers to eager students who have proved willing customers. They sell term papers written by graduate students or teaching assistants who, for a fee, will do the research necessary to provide the students with term papers that are guaranteed to achieve passing grades. The educational process has become meaningless to these students. (The process is too widespread to conclude that only lazy students turn to these ready made papers.) The papers are, in reality, as relevant to education as the grades, computerized tests, and robot-like lectures. All are tools of artifice. If a student seriously tries to work for change, he is often told that the institution must proceed as its own lugubrious pace, capable of reforming only through the accession and consent of men whose self-perpetuation is directly opposite in instinct to reform. If a university (or any other institution) loses its capacity to change, grow, and evolve, it will ultimately sow the seeds of its own destruction.

All of this serves as a preference to the realization that the majority of student activists are not "reformers." A difference exists between reform (i.e., change for the better) and abolition (destruction). Author John Coyne, has suggested that today's colleges are no places for reformers. Unfortunately, he is right.

The student who wishes to work for legitimate reform on campus is usually ignored. Instead, attention is diverted to the militant agitators who strive to take advantage of existing grievances on campus and turn these grievances to their own ends. Ultimately, they are not concerned with the welfare of the students or the well-being of the campus. They are concerned with their own self-interest and the achievement of power. If some legitimate grievances may be used as a means for campus agitation, well and good. If not, they can easily create some grievances that may be used as a point of departure. Needless to say, they do not have to search very long or hard to find these existing grievances.

In evaluating the state of affairs in the schools, two unfortunate tendencies are easily discernible. One is the appalling tendency of some persons to deny the reality of legitimate weakness in the present ways of administering colleges and universities.

The second tendency is the deliberate effort to ignore the existence of radicals who eschew personal responsibility in their own passionate pursuit of power.

When well-meaning, but naïve men and women abandon common sense to talk about different forms of authority, they choose to ignore the obvious fact that in any society, order must come from somewhere or someone. The youthful revolutionaries capture public sympathy because they are glorified and glamorized in the press, Order as an alternative to chaos seems preferable, if man is to escape the law of the jungle.

The greatest difficulty in understanding the problems which have dominated college campuses over the last decade lies in recognizing the root causes of these dilemmas. Discussions about whether or not the campuses have quieted down since the late 60's are superfluous.

Many of us are tempted to approach the whole relationship between students and administrators as we approach the relationships between citizens and their government: through generalizations. It is easy enough to dichotomize, to blithely assume that these questions may be resolved through an "either/or" approach. Either the students are right, or the administrations must be right. Either the schools are doing a good job or they are not. Either the campuses are quiet or they are in turmoil. These neat assumptions provide us with convenient mental escape hatches; they facilitate our ignoring the primary question at hand, the basic purposes of colleges and universities. An in-depth examination of this question invariably compels us to ask some hard questions about the whole educational process.

In the 1970's, students have tended to concentrate more upon practical problems, such as unemployment, than on emotional political issues. Ironically, it is the practical and pragmatic crisis which most clearly reflects the true essence of what has been wrong on our college campuses. Thousands of students deeply resent graduating from school, only to find that they have little or no training for the specific job market on hand. Education has been traditionally marketed in this country as a means of achieving upward economic mobility.

The difficulty is that we must contend with imagery. The advocate of reversing the sexes doesn't talk about what he is really suggesting; he attacks a straw man, equal employment denial. The advocate of the sexual revolution attacks another straw man, Victorian morality, as if this were a problem today.

In talking about questions involving the generations, proponents of the youth culture offer us an either/or choice. We can accept their assorted ideas, propositions, and theories, or run the risk of being labeled Archie Bunker, ignoramuses, or know-nothings.

The key to shattering stereotypical interpretations of social change is to cut through the jargon to the essence of the arguments. It is pompous and presumptuous for anyone to talk about "the young point of view", with stress on the word "the". There is no single point of view identified with young people. More important, it is a disservice to our society to label ideas "young" or "old", since these labels add false validity to arguments and positions which should stand on their own.

The basic stereotype calls for us to compare the views of liberated, progressive, intelligent young people and their repressed, inhibited elders. Once we have accepted the basic notion, it is simple enough to make judgements on a whole variety of questions without ever really understanding what we are talking about.

The student who attends college may think primarily in terms of increasing his earning power. True, he will read the lofty sentiments in the catalogue about acquainting himself with mankind's cultural heritage. But we may ask ourselves how many students would attend a university if they were told its exclusive purpose were unrelated to career preparation.

So the unemployed graduate may ask bitterly, "Why did I go to college at all? What was I really doing there? " He may more directly be inclined to demand an explanation from his professors, and vicariously, the administration. What exactly do college administrations think is the basic purpose of education?

The incisive mind will quickly recognize that our problems are never solved merely by pinning convenient nametags on the heroes and villains of a campus melodrama. An objective assessment of the 1960's campus violence will more than likely reveal faults on both sides of the question. There has been so much attention focused on whether or not the students or administration were to blame for what happened, we have seldom considered the possibility that both elements were responsible, but in different ways.

Administrations and professors have traditionally encouraged students to regard themselves as an elite group. Small children tend traditionally to like what they know, to suspect the unfamiliar, to mistrust the unknown. Teenagers are most prone to follow fads. Current trends in education have encouraged teachers to foster such tastes in young people. William Ronwer, Jr., Professor of Education at the University of California at Berkley told a National Education Association conference that, under the current system, "the only kinds of children for whom school is congenial are those who have a bent for reading and arithmetic." He went on to recommend that children be free to select only subjects that interest them and in which they do well.

The danger of this attitude is clear, especially when introduced during the elementary school years and carried forward through adolescence. By the time a boy or girl is ready for college, he has been encouraged consistently to think that his ideas and tastes alone are important; admittedly, there would be an equal danger in denying the natural creative impulses of children or recognizing their own sense of individuality. But in an educational world totally dominated by permissiveness, it is the former, not the latter, which poses the essential problem.

Students who have no desire to learn can rationalize behavior as a means of "expressing their true selves." All of this will be applauded by those who follow the fashionable popular psychological jargon of the day. Consider the case of Anne Roiphe, who began to have doubts about the way in which her daughter was being educated. As a mother, she recognized that something was wrong when her daughter "went on peace marches with friends, cared about the poor and the suffering, wore torn bluejeans, went to parties where

they turned out the lights, but could never remember where
her math book had last been seen." Her parents were concerned about her school, which devoted itself more to discussions of potential and differing maturity rates than
homework turned in on time. So they arranged for her to
transfer to a school with an old-fashioned approach to
educational fundamentals. The girls wear skirts or dresses to
class, the boys wear jackets, and address their teachers as
"Sir". They stand when an adult enters the room.

When the parents visited their daughter, they were in for
a surprise. Far from being bored by the school's emphasis on
individual achievement, their sophisticated teenager was
excited by the athletic competitions, the awards for classroom accomplishment, the emphasis on honor, morality, and
individual responsibility. Anne Roiphe, ready to say good-
bye to John Dewey, and "Hello" to Cotton Mather, quickly
re-examined her own concepts of education. "The school's
faculty members think in terms of meeting challenges, performing according to external standards, and somehow it
amounts to a profound kind of caring for the child", she
wrote.

As a graduate of Sarah Lawrence who believed in a
maximum of freedom, Anne Roiphe found it necessary to
conclude that choice and freedom place specialized burdens
on a child. She went on to observe that children feel secure
because adults take it upon themselves to explain what is
right and what is wrong and why there may be consequences
for doing something.

Not all parents, of course, are willing to take the time or
trouble to really examine the philosophical basis of permissiveness. If they do, they invariably find that far from
providing children with greater freedom, a total absence of
authority simply chains the young irrevocably to their own
sense of inadequacy. They compensate for this by rebelling.

College professors encourage another type of elitism. Too
many academicians, as a result of their training, become
experts regarding a subject of microcosmic proportions. They
may find it necessary to learn everything there is to know
about a tiny, insignificant subject. Since graduate schools

place emphasis upon specialization, the college professor may indeed become an expert in something. But the human temptation is there; professors can easily assume that their real or imaginary expertise in one subject may be transferred to all subjects. Since the world seldom recognizes their universal expertise in all subjects, they may succumb to the temptation to become frustrated. This frustration may reveal itself in the form of a latent belief in their own superiority, a quality which they recognize even if the world does not.

The student who becomes involved in an undergraduate curriculum is thus encouraged to follow two leads; his own, which may lack a sense of direction, and that of his professors, which may go in the wrong direction. The qualities which schools are supposed to encourage are imagination, creativity, and the inquiring mind. Yet it is very likely that the inquiring mind will immediately be asking all the wrong questions on campus. He may reject the rote discipline of outmoded teaching methods, or see through the pretentious academic jargon which masks incompetence. He may object to excessive emphasis on paperwork and forms, the mainstay of the campus bureaucracy. Most of all, he may be inclined to commit himself to positions or issues which are in disfavor with the majority of professors.

So the universities, which have encouraged the individual student to have a high regard for his own thinking, may find themselves the targets of his wrath. The enigma is that the student who recognizes legitimate grievances may have no real means of expressing himself. The universities have tended to function very much like the nursery schools which let children do whatever they want. Responsible leadership, the type found at the school where Anne Roiphe sent her daughter, may provide a sense of direction. Yet the typical college may be permissive regarding the content and essence of education, and rigid regarding the paper requirements. The student who may do best at college is the one with a preference for basketweaving, social relationships, and seminars in political protest. He may care little for fundamentals, but if his papers are in order, if his files are kept in the proper places, if his forms are filled out, he may find it easy to adjust to the environment. Professors will encourage him to assume that what he knows or likes is more important than what anyone else knows; if he plays the game, indulges in an intellectual *pas de deux* with his professors, he can join the critical elite. Like its other members, he will be frustrated by society's lack of recognition for his self-estimated importance.

The student who rebels and rejects the specific mechanics of obtaining a degree will be regarded as an intellectual outcast by members of the academic establishment.

For too long, we have rationalized regarding the true nature of campus conflict, characterizing it as a rivalry between administrators who believe in something vaguely described as "the Establishment", and rebellious students seeking to overthrow it. Yet the greater part of the "establishment" has been both pompous and permissive, eager to encourage the young to follow their own anarchistic instincts, horrified to reap the dubious rewards of their theories put into practice. The greater part of the student population has been encouraged to foster the prejudices and pontifical notions of a pampered elite. Confusing rhetoric with philosophy, arrogance with erudition, education with intelligence, the students have all the qualities of spoiled children. Perhaps it is easiest to understand what happened on our campuses by realizing that professors and students often behave like permissive parents and spoiled children: both are wrong.

There are two little recognized minorities on campus: Professors who stress fundamentals, whose expertise is practical, who fail to be awed by the jargon and rhetoric. Students with inquiring minds who recognize that the schools are far from perfect, but who thirst for knowledge. The true teacher cannot fail to be angered by the appearance of students who regard themselves as part of a critical elite, frustrated and superior, ready to assert themselves and their own meager perspectives at anyone's expense. The true student cannot fail to be infuriated by the preponderance of academicians who are what one caustic professor described as educated fools.

The true teachers and pupils will not be attracted to the idea of political paranoia. They recognize that the creation of a mythical monster, "The Establishment", is motivated by the desires of frustrated men and women, students and professors alike, to provide themselves with a whipping boy. Anyone really interested in teaching knows that the process is an art, involving the transmission of ideas, the communication and stimulating discourse that can only take place in a classroom. But these noble goals cannot be achieved without hard fundamentals, without a tough-minded recognition that in the classroom, there must be a leader. He does not have to carry a whip and chair, like a lion tamer entering the cage of the circus. But there can be no question as to who is teacher and who is pupil. In turn, the teacher has the responsibility to lead, not to pontificate, to read dull lecture notes, to put in enough time to earn his salary, and go through the motions of the teaching process.

The unsung heroes of the campus crisis are those teachers and pupils who have engaged in activities upon which there has been placed too little stress in recent years: teaching and learning.

These are the real purposes of colleges and universities, and unless we revitalize our emphasis upon them, the campus will fall prey once again to the assault of those whose interest lies not in the medium of education, but in the achievement of their own power.

VI.

ADOLESCENCE BEGINS AT FORTY

Nothing is so easy as to deceive one's self; for what we wish, we readily believe; but such expectations are often inconsistent with the reality of things . . . . **Demosthenes**

No wise man ever wished to be younger . . . . **Johnathan Swift**

One of the most bizarre and fascinating aspects of the generation gap is the role played by adults who sympathize, ostensibly, with the younger generation. (In reality, they are expressing empathy with a selected segment of the younger generation.)

The nation has an abundance of persons, many of whom are prominent and influential to varying degrees, who are only too eager to express their enthusiasm for "the kids," and their concurrent disdain for the critics who express disapproval of youth's current fads and fashions.

The key to understanding these persons and their peculiar behavior lies in realization of the essence of middle-age, Barbara Fried, in her book, *The Middle Age Crisis*, suggests that the over-forty adult is not unlike the fourteen-year-old. He needs to prove himself. The middle-aged businessman is faced, for the first time in his life, with the prospect of competing against men who regard him as old, even if this term is absurd when applied to a man who is forty. Suddenly, he finds the role that has always been his usurped by others. The middle-aged mother may find her children growing up, with an apparent erosion of her usefulness. Her maternal instinct may be as great as ever, but its satisfaction may be sadly lacking. Both middled-aged parents may need reassurance that they are still attractive to members of the opposite sex.

One does not need a diploma in psychology to see that one alternative reaction to the crisis of middle-age is a resolution to prove one's self. Adolescents' awkwardness and lack of assurance have been the target of comedians and cartoonists for years. The fourteen-year-old boy may strut, swagger, and be predictably overzealous in efforts to publically demonstrate his masculinity. (He is not a man, of course, and when he tries to behave in a manner that he thinks is masculine, he succeeds only in becoming a caricature.)

When mature, he no longer has to boast that he is old enough to shave. Everyone else his age also shaves, and he has undoubtedly come to regard shaving as a daily chore which exemplifies no particular aura of masculine expression. A mature girl does not have to develop herself in seventeen layers of cosmetics and lipsticks in order to appear "mature," as she may have tried to do when she was fourteen. She no longer needs to try to prove she is a "woman," because she is one.

At forty, however, the middle-aged man and woman have a good deal to prove. The trend has reversed. Instead of trying to prove they are mature (as teenagers wishing their childhoods were behind them), they want to identify with the young (in order to prove that their futures are ahead of them). The grass is always greener! We may sympathize with this dilemma, and even understand it. But the desire of a forty-year-old man to prove he is still twenty is not unlike the desire of a teenager to prove he is a man: in both instances, the artificiality of the masquerade dulls the senses, confuses one's values, and in a discussion of the generation gap, utterly unglues one's sense of equilibrium

The "middle-aged adolescent," if we may assign that term, is easily recognized. In his speech, his choice of clothing, and most important of all, his expressed attitudes, he

tries to emulate the young men and women that he identifies as "progressive." The teenage adolescent will boast
about shaving, smoking, sex, and his disdain for traditions.
Except for shaving, the middle-aged adolescent will boast
about the same things.

In dealing with members of the younger generation, the
over-forty adult may encounter boys and girls who do not
flaunt their youth. The young man may wear a suit and tie,
or favor short sideburns and neatly clipped hair. The girls
may prefer dresses to pants, and even demonstrate an inclination toward hats, gloves, and a hairstyle that does not
resemble a wind-blown scarecrow.

If these persons are college students, they are aware of
their own youth. It is unnecessary for them to advertise
what is obvious to them. Curiously enough, they do not
regard themselves as stodgy, narrow-minded, or unsophisticated. But they do not deliberately dress or behave in a way
which is identified as "youthful rebellion" by middle-aged
persons. (In reality, these young men and women are non-
conforming in the face of mass conformity which pervades
the unwashed Woodstock society.)

If a bearded, sideburned young man in bell bottoms and a
see-through shirt walks into the room, the middle-aged
person identifies him erroneously as a "non-conformist."
Simultaneously, this young man may challenge many of the
values and ideas previously held by the over-forty adult.

An objective reaction to this person's appearance might
be the assumption that he looks or behaves like a court
jester (if he indeed behaves that way). This does not mean
every young man who dresses according to the above description is a fool; it does not mean that he is a sage either.

The middle-aged adolescent, however, does not want to
identify with anyone or anything which reinforces his own
values, because he is basically insecure in his own personal
and social role. He does not like the role of the "stuffed
shirt," a role which the unwashed protagonist may be eager
to assign to him. *He* is accustomed to being thought of as
dynamic, progressive, and young. His over-forty instinct,
therefore, is not to defend his own ideas or opinions, but to

join in some way, the most glaring self-advertisement for youth and change. By joining the pack, he reinforces his own self-image as part of the youth movement gaining control rather than as part of the middle-aged society that seems to be destined for oblivion.

Perhaps the greatest source of his hostility is the conservative young man and woman. (Conservative is used here in a non-political context, with reference to a belief that change is not progress, necessarily.) The radical who wants to achieve sudden or abrupt changes finds a willing ally in the would-be twenty-year-old, wishing for all the world that he was not forty (or fifty). The middle-aged adolescent is scared and frightened that the world will pass him by. He is determined to prove to the young men demanding changes that he is one of them. He wants to say, "All right, I'm a reasonable fellow. I'm not like the other old fogies."

Fogy, a four-letter word, is perhaps the only obscenity left in the society of apologists for the youth cult. The over-forty man or woman is often tempted to discard his common sense, because the overpowering stimulus affecting his reason (and his relative security regarding sex and power, depending on whether one is a follower of Freud or Jung) is his desire to identify with youth. It behooves us to recognize that he does not identify with all youth; young men and women who may oppose violent upheavals in society do not reinforce his own youth image.

They are trying to preserve what may be constructive in our social and political systems. But they too are brushed aside by social and political revolutionaries who invoke their claims of "youthful idealism" as an excuse to advance their goals. The middle-aged adolescent, who could exert some intelligent influence, does not. Instead, he allows his fear to blind him. He is so desperately concerned about advertising his receptive attitude toward "change" and "progress," that he does not bother to ask himself if specific ideas or proposals really imply positive change, or even if the slogans or rhetoric employed by some members of the youth cult are really grounded in substance. He turns a hostile eye toward the young men and women who seem to be resisting these

changes, even against the agitations of an assortment of
groups who are part of their own generation. These young
men and women are forgotten Americans. They are ignored
by their contemporaries, whose very claim to legitimacy
implies as a prerequisite their assertion that they represent
all youth. They also receive the antipathy of the middle-aged
adolescent, who regards any effort to identify him with resistance to change, even detrimental change, as a meretri-
cious threat to his youth image. As we shall see in a
moment, the error is fatal.

A relatively simple demonstration of this principle may be
found merely by examining some instances in which middle-
aged adults take curiously incongruous positions on controversies involving youth. We shall also see that these same
middle-aged adolescents are perfectly willing to ignore or
oppose the wishes or ideals of young people who do not
reinforce their own youth image.

Consider, for a moment, the most obvious example of the
generation gap, dress. In various parts of the country, high
school principals have been besieged with requests to abolish
dress codes, the rules that restrict clothing and grooming of
students. In Beverly Hills, California, one of the nations
most affluent school districts, the dress code was first re-
pealed and then reinstated. No self-respecting college president or dean would dream of imposing any restrictions
whatsoever on the dress or hairstyles of students.

The most curious aspect of this situation is the position
of parents. Efforts by schools or academic administrators to
impose restrictions on hair length or the more outrageous
trends in juvenile fashion are often interpreted as efforts to
impose the Establishment on the free spirit of youth.

When teachers prepared to protest the obvious efforts of
adolescents to emulate their assorted idols, usually the long
haired unwashed variety, they were in for a surprise. Mini-
skirted mothers, eager to reinforce their youth-image, heard
the call to arms. Middle-aged fathers, often balding, with
skin-tight shirts emphasizing their pot-bellies, but determined
to sprout chin-length sideburns, were ready to do battle.
High-school principals were not able to depend on their

faculties however, because mini-skirted music teachers and male teachers with flared pants were hardly in a position to argue with parents.

Similarly, middle-aged principals were joining the bandwagon to the consternation of their superiors. The cycle, ludicrous as it may seem, was taking its toll. Why is this wrong? Doesn't this merely represent a change in fashion or a change in styles? Are these forms of dress and grooming merely offensive to little old ladies in tennis shoes, longing for the music of Lawrence Welk and the politics of McKinley? Not in the least!

When the parents and teachers follow suit, they are becoming followers, not leaders. A popular television commercial for a dishwashing detergent is a case in point. The commercial features a woman who squeals with glee to a somewhat befuddled looking acquaintance, while standing next to her own son, "I'm not his date – I'm his mother! " The implication is obvious. Madison Avenue is prepackaging a youth-image. If mother and father are busily trying to look like junior's dates, why should they be surprised when junior cultivates slobbism?

The motion picture and television industries are presently dominated by the world's largest army of middle-aged adolescents. Although studio personnel prefer to remain anonymous (they fear reprisals for even the most innocuous statement made about their superiors), the author has been advised constantly that studio executives prefer to emphasize hiring of employees who maintain a youth image. (This is indeed a pernicious form of discrimination.) One department head prefers employees who apply for their jobs in purple shirts, flared pants, and shoulder-length hair. Suits and ties are Establishment, and consequently, as obsolete as yesterday's cancelled checks.

Consider the following, which was reported in *The Beverly Hills Independent*:

A resident of Beverly Hills told the city council that he caught a boy and a girl having sexual intercourse in broad daylight on his front lawn. He resolved the problem by turning the sprinklers on. And to his consternation, the girl's mother telephoned him and bawled him out for getting her daughter wet.

The episode seems amusing, certainly with its comical aspects. But the greater issue is that this particular mother would not dream of criticizing her daughter's morals because this would seem "narrow," "conservative," or "old-fashioned."

Kenneth Clark, world renowned art critic, has defined "courtesy" as "the ritual by which men avoid hurting other people's feelings." Courtesy, along with polished speech and an emphasis on the social manifestation of manners, is the antithesis of the obscenity which permeates the youth cult. If courtesy and refinement are meaningful, it is because they possess intrinsic worth. They dignify man and expand his humanity in the process. A civilization cannot be expected to evolve (or change for the better) by fostering the ideal that no form of behavior is any better or worse than any other form of behavior. Egalitarianism cannot be carried to its furthest extreme without becoming authoritarian in itself. If obscenity is just as "right" or "proper" in society as any other form of self-expression, concurrently we may assume that other forms of self-expression are no better or worse for social progress than obscenity. To object to the self-perpetuation of any form of behavior becomes a form of restriction. But an absence of any restrictions leads to the assumption that morality (or the desirability of prevalence of some elements over others) is meaningless. If "right" or "wrong" become meaningless, man becomes concurrently amoral. He reverts to the law of the jungle.

In no way does the abandonment of a permissive or conciliatory attitude toward obscenity imply a subliminal yearning for censorship, abolition of free speech, or any other totalitarian practices. An unfortunate reality of modern-day society is in evidence when persons who denounce public obscenity are labeled "prudes." To accept the implication that any group of men or women regard the free and unrestricted use of obscenity as part of their culture is to merely encourage the most irresponsible and tiny minority of rabble rousers who seek to use "obscenity" as one additional means of advancing their own gains. If Johnny turns up in the classroom using four-letter words as an essential part of his vocabulary, he needs to learn in no uncertain terms the reasons why certain words are objectionable in polite society. It is high time that the middle-aged adolescents stop applauding the normalization of obscenity. It is also high time that we stop assigning "subtle meanings" and sociological implications to the pathetic utterances of those persons who best express their frustrations through the use of four-letter words. Teachers or parents who encourage little boys and girls to express themselves in the vocabularies of the gutter perform a massive disservice to society. Ultimately, these children will grow into uncouth primitives, only too ready to tell their teachers, parents, and the rest of society where to go. This will be accomplished in the basest of terms. Vulgarity is not "honesty." Crudity is not "self-expression." Obscenity is not "freedom." The middle-aged adolescent who cannot tell the difference is a sadly befuddled individual.

There have been voices in the wilderness, but too often these voices have been silenced by ridicule. Apologists for the youth cult dispose of their critics in a neat and thoroughly efficient way; they ignore them. If a critical voice is raised by someone who has yet to achieve a substantial identity in the academic or literary world (usually a young man or woman), the criticism is dismissed as immature prattle. (Apologists for the youth cult believe that young people should be "understood," but this courtesy does not extend to those young persons whose expression does not reinforce the apologists' own views.) If the objections are voiced by someone over thirty, he can be easily written off as an old-fashioned antiquarian whose stuffy prejudices prevent him from appreciating the subtleties of a Ringo Starr banging away on his drum, or the deep socio-political implications of John Lennon and Yoko Ono being photographed in the nude for a record jacket.

Grace and Fred M. Hechinger saw the handwriting on the wall in their remarkably perceptive book, *Teen-Age Tyranny*. Written during the early 1960's, the book deals primarily with the teenage society of the late 1950's and early 1960's, emphasizing aspects of the youth culture prior to the advent of hippies, mass drug addiction, the post-Beatle era of rock music, and widespread political millitancy. But they recognized, even at this early date, that the mushrooming teenage culture was growing in an ill-advised way.

We know all too well where these trends have led. The Hechingers trace the beginnings of the problem to permissive parents and teachers. They comment, "The trouble started when all forms of self-expression were put on an equal level of importance and value. The child who just sneared paints across the pad was seen as expressing himself as usefully as the child who showed the beginnings of a sense of color and pattern." They go on to observe, "The youngster who had something original to say was given no more recognition than the classmate who merely babbled for the sake of the sound of his voice, or worse, his quickly recognized power to gain attention and disrupt the show. Ultimately, this view led to the extreme perversion of the progressive idea — the theory that ungrammatical idiom is just as good and as expressive of the real self as correct usage. In fact, there were some who began to deride the "correct" expression as society-dictated and therefore destructive of individual expression."

By now, of course, the idea that non-achievement merits the same rewards as achievement, coupled with the assertion that every manifestation of self-expression is "equal" has borne rotten fruit. Obscenity is glorified as "art," or "literature." Rock groups are assumed to possess profound insight regarding our social ills, equating their simplistic lyrics with philosophical wisdom (and musical expertise). Political violence is equated with "free speech." Immorality is justified as "doing your own thing." Because no one "judges" anyone else, moral behavior or artistic achievement are no longer entitled to the encouragement of society. Like all good theories, the concept of encouraging self-expression can be self-defeating when carried to its ultimate extreme. When someone criticizes this, he runs the risk of facing an angry army of critics, with pencils poised or tar and feathers ready, as the case may be. He is immediately accused of expressing desires for a return to the authoritarian form of education administered by a severe taskmaster who regularly exhibits compassion worthy of a composite Mr. Murdstone and Simon Legree. This is puerile nonsense.

If a child wants to race around the classroom destroying other people's property, he needs to be taught that this particular desire for self-expression violates someone else's rights. He must learn that the other children have rights too, including the right not to have their property destroyed. If students want to protest any policy of the government, they have peaceful and responsible means to do so. When they destroy property, throw rocks and bottles at policemen, or brutally intimidate other students who do not agree with them, they are not merely protesting, they are trampling on the rights of others. Apologists for the youth cult are willing to recognize the "right" of a student to break windows, but not the "right" of a man to live in a house without worrying about the possibility of rocks sailing through his window. They are quick to demand that all cultural expressions be received "equally." They deny, therefore, the right of recognition to a man who has devoted long and hard hours of work to his chosen discipline. If two men write music or author books or paint pictures, and one is exceptionally gifted, the gifted man deserves recognition.

To deny him recognition on the grounds that such a response discriminates against the less gifted is utter nonsense. All men are not created equal in talent or ability. "Equality" implies an equality of opportunity coupled with a recognition of the basic dignity and humanity that belongs to all men. But individuals do not possess the same capacities for achievement, any more than the validity of their moral standards or personal ideals is the same. The most dangerous aspect of middle-aged adolescence is the peculiar notion that society can function without any standards or morals.

Of course any attempt to impose standards or restrictions on any element in society will seem oppressive to those persons who are restricted. What the apologists and middle-aged adolescents fail to perceive is that granting equal worth to any idea or any achievement is to negate the processes of human thought that are essential to an ordered society. Charles Reich might be upset by the use of the word "ordered," because the use of the word is distorted by apologists for the youth cult to imply an Orwellian, totalitarian state. But a society with no standards or restrictions ultimately leads to a totalitarian state; concurrently it encourages dictatorship by a mob, and ultimately, by the mob's leaders.

Concerned adults must realize that by the time a child reaches college age, parents cannot suddenly expect him to develop into a responsible citizen. The permissive attitude must be altered or eschewed when he is still at an early age. What may be mild permissiveness toward the young child can degenerate into an obsequious "pals" policy toward the teenager and culminate in the spineless acquiescence of the middle-aged adolescents toward their young adult counterparts. The Hechingers criticize books, by authors like William C. Menninger, which offer advice to parents and teenagers, implying the family should be a "democratic unit," with junior encouraged to have an equal voice. They declare, "Having been pals rather than parents before, they now become a mixture of part-time providers, part-time social workers. But while adolescent hostilities do exist, of course, and should not be given exaggerated importance, the teenager who finds rudeness and disrespect accepted and explained away as a natural phenomenon merely revels in his victory over adult society. There are even strong indications that adolescents are testing their power at least as much as they are rebelling, and they fully expect and want to have a limit set for their actions."

Similarly, Dr. Harriett B. Randall, psychiatrist with the Pasadena Child Guidance Clinic and former medical director for the Los Angeles City School district, advises us, "Giving a child things, but denying him yourself may result in not giving him appropriate controls, or guidance. Substituting things for love, or thinking that things will represent love, fellowship, and contact, is a great mistake." Dr. Randall also says that children want leaders who offer protection, stability and guidance. She says that children do not want parents who are "pals."

Of course, young adults are not children. But middle-aged adolescents, seeking reassurance from the young adults that the forty-year-old imitators of the youth cult are "pals," check their common sense at the door.

Perhaps the most glaring discrepancy in the illogic that governs the theories advanced in the *Greening of America* is the inability to recognize the lack of constructive alternatives in the youth culture. K. Ross Toole, Professor of History at the University of Montana, has denounced the "tyranny of spoiled brats" and what he terms the "pusillanimous capitulation" to a small minority in the younger generation. Toole continues, "By virtue of what right, by what accomplishment should teenagers wet behind the ears and utterly without the benefit of having lived long enough to have either judgment or wisdom become the sages of our time?" He goes on to declare, "Common courtesy and a regard for the opinions of others are not merely decoration on the pie crust of society — they are the heart of the pie. Too many 'youngsters' are egocentric boors. They will not listen and discuss; they will only shout down and throw rocks. Society has classically ostracized arrogance without the backing of demonstrable accomplishment."

In this context, Toole is functioning as an unofficial spokesman for a sizeable community of middle-aged adults. He made these statements because he believes, with considerable justification, that the parental generation has abdicated its responsibilities of leadership. The "older generation," as it is often euphemistically described, has indeed come to grips with some of the great problems that plague civilization: Poverty, racism, war, and disease. Great scientific advances and medical discoveries have provided new hope for millions. Thousands of middle-aged persons possess the same desires for peace, prosperity, and universal goodwill that ostensibly emanate from the youth culture.

Poet Karl Shapiro expressed a concurring viewpoint when he said, "The American adulation of the child mentality leads to an industrialized hedonism on one hand, and a chauvinistic psychology of greed on the other. In advertising, anyone over the age of twenty-one or twenty-five is portrayed as an idiot who has got behind in the science and commerce of rejuvenation."

The "older generation" suffers from an abundance of individuals who seek to wear their guilt on their sleeves, eager to advertise their "responsibility" for all the ills of the world. War, racism, and poverty are complex problems. They were not invented by the previous generation, any more than a desire for solutions to these problems was created by the present generation. Ironically, too many young persons (and their middle-aged adolescent apologists) are willing to condemn *en masse* an entire generation of mature adults while failing to recognize the individual failings of their own contemporaries.

Toole advises parents to back the vast majority of young men and women who do not require apology. He admits, however, that this procedure is "too direct for those who seek to employ Freudian analysis, too positive for 'academic senates' who long for philosophical debate, and too prosaic for those who seek orgiastic condemnation."

Most apologists for the youth cult are quick to advertise the mistakes of their own generation. Indeed, the parents of today's young men and women have made countless errors, like all generations. They are also far more capable of recognizing these errors than previous generations. Nothing presents a greater example of the inconsistency of middle-aged adolescents than their ability to denounce the "mistakes" of their own generation, while failing to even recognize the existence of these same "mistakes" in the generation they defend. (In truth, they defend only a vocal minority within this generation.)

What is the answer to these middle-aged adolescents as they offer the unwashed minority their eager approbation? The answer is not new. It is neither surprising nor innovative. The answer is a return to the principles, a departure from which has been responsible for the current condition.

Adults must stop saying, "Me, too." Children are not leaders, although they can exhibit qualities of leadership. When they do, they should be encouraged to apply those qualities in constructive ways; not because, as Charles Reich would have it, society "knows what is best"; not because one element of society seeks to impose its will on another; rather, because human behavior has intrinsic worth or lack of worth. College students are not children. They are young men and women, and should behave in responsible ways. "Responsible" does not mean that they should abandon ideals or accept compromises with their desires, if they have them, to improve the world. The world can do very nicely with some persons who want to make the world a better place to live. "Responsible" means that one does not tread on the rights of others or tear down the foundations of Western civilization and American society offering nothing but mindless anarchy or aimless chaos in return. Families are not democracies in which junior's bedtime or his right to use the family car is put to a vote. This does not mean that parents should refuse to communicate with their children, or that one generation should be immune from criticism by the other. But "communication" does not imply acquiescence, and criticism is not a process whereby one generation appeases the whims and caprices of a vocal element of the other, for purposes of reinforcing its own youth image.

It is high time adults stop worrying about recapturing their own lost youth and start behaving like mature, sensible people. If the younger generation wants to abolish poverty, racism, war, and desease, they will find many welcome allies in persons of all ages. Perhaps, however, remembering some old (and still valid) references to persons in glass houses, vocal advocates of the youth cult and their middle-aged apologists would do well to start within their own ranks.

Consider the ramifications of constructive action. Otis Carney was a successful Beverly Hills television writer who had a wife, three sons, professional esteem, and considerable affluence. At the age of forty-six, he began seeking a "new lease on life" when he moved his family to a cattle ranch in

Wyoming. The Carneys began adapting to their new lives as ranchers.

Carney was in a position to purchase a ranch, but even a large cattle spread represented a considerable departure from the life the family had previously known. Carney re-examined his own priorities. He decided that the life he really wanted could be best obtained in another way. But his family approached the matter in a constructive way. He did not become a middle-aged hippie, a polemicist for the drug culture, or dress like a court jester and buy a one-way ticket to Berkeley. In his book, *New Lease on Life*, Otis Carney recounts the episode of a long-haired youth who arrived at the ranch with some friends, seeking work. The young men rebelled when asked to cut their hair, even though shoulder-length hair is distinctly inappropriate in rural Wyoming society. The boys decided to return East. But following a lecture by Mrs. Carney, one of the young men walked at least twenty miles returning to the ranch. The writer's wife had challenged the young men's assertion that they were only "kids" and did not find it necessary to accept responsibility. Although his companions went East, the young man went to work on the ranch, cut his hair, and did his job well. Otis Carney observed, "I don't know if we helped that boy, or set him back in his search for himself. But I do believe in a few weeks he grew toward manhood, simply because somebody had challenged him."

Apologists for the youth cult would be up in arms, of course, because Carney, according to their way of reasoning, should have grown shoulder-length hair himself. The purpose of this behavior would have been to demonstrate to the youths that the rancher understood "what the kids want." These middle-aged adolescents do not realize that the "kids" often don't know what they want.

If Otis Carney's position on this particular issue is an example of one basic reaction in microcosm, the other side of the coin is equally valid as a case in point. Larry Uttal, President of Bell Records, is more unhappy than a child who has been made to doubt the authenticity of Santa Claus. Larry Uttal understands his son, and he wants other parents to realize that they obviously don't understand theirs. "I think if a parent is really in a position where he cannot stand his youngster's musical taste, then he's in a position where, at least subconsicously, he cannot stand his youngster," he declares. Uttal, once an unsuccessful songwriter, determined that he would "understand" the music and lyrics that appealed to his teenage son. He read about the new teenage idols, copied their lyrics down on paper, and finally, like the man who learned to love Big Brother in *1984*, Larry Uttal appreciated rock, "If you turn off your child's culture, it's the same thing as turning off your child," he declares. If we apply this remarkable piece of psychological profundity, imagine the possibilities. Junior, let us say, may choose to enjoy pornographic films, hallucinogenic drugs, or an assortment of vices. (Junior is too sophisticated for baseball or a good novel.) Suddenly, the parent who "turns off his child's culture," is ruining his child's life. If junior wants to study depravity, how dare his parent refuse to "understand"? Depravity may seem to be a strong word, you say, melodramatic and overemotional. Consider for a moment the "cultural" posture of Ray Davies and Alice Cooper. Davies is an English rock musician who calls his group The Kinks. Davies has been known to empty a can of beer on the front row of fans in the audience. The fans ostensibly reach up for the beer as baseball fans reach for a fly ball. Rock columnist and apologist Robert Hilburn calls Davies "one of the most literate and valuable writers who ever put his mind to the business of rock'n'roll." But Hilburn, who indicates quickly his own level of taste, admits that Davies is not as elaborate as Alice Cooper. A long-haired *man*, Cooper describes his group's achievements with glee. "We get our audiences so crazy. One night in Detroit there was a motorcycle gang that was so stoned! I have an inflated rabbit. As I threw it out into the crowd, I yelled, 'Kill it! ' One of the motorcycle gang started stabbing it with a knife. The gang charged up on stage. Police were called, but the motorcycle gang scared the cops out. That is entertainment! " Cooper chops up baby dolls and stages a mock hanging of himself as part of his act, which emphasizes fright and violence as part of "the

rock art form." Lest we conclude that the young man with
the strange name is sadly lacking credentials for sanity, we
are reminded that off stage Cooper devotes considerable time
to his investments and financial profits, and to his country
home in Connecticut. A minister's son, he keeps his real
identity a secret: This is an example of what Larry Uttal
wants us to "understand." He says, "Just appreciate your
children, and their musical likes, and take time to understand why they like what they like. If they could put the
new math on a record, they might conquer the world's fiscal
problems."

Fortunately, Larry Uttal, Robert Hilburn, and persons of
similar "insight" have been content to devote their full time
to ruining the record industry. They have not started to turn
their talents to the world's economic ills — yet!

This does not represent an implication that all "young
ideas" are as banal as an Alice Cooper performance. But the
inability to distinguish between sincere youthful idealism and
the psychological insecurity of pampered, spoiled brats can
be fatal. The middle-aged adolescents is typified by the
parent who cannot see the Alice Cooper phenomenon as a
form of sickness. Teenagers and post-adolescents, obviously
tired of television or films, need new "thrills" or "kicks."
This was not always so.

Arthur Prager, in his book about 1930's and 1940's
Rascals at Large, recalls, "Society was definitely not permissive, sexually or otherwise. Youthful activities were strictly
supervised and controlled. Pleasure was rare and hard to
find. This toughened us. We learned to find happiness in
small inexpensive things."

Today's culture is neither small nor inexpensive. The
parent whose sole motivation is to "understand" his child's
"culture," which he assumes in advance to be meritorious, is
in for a rude awakening. Certainly young people have legitimate concerns about war, pollution, peace, prosperity, poverty, and other important issues facing society.

Thousands of adults, despite publicity to the contrary,
share these concerns. But to pervert and distort legitimate
hopes and aspirations of some young people as an excuse to

grant any manifestation of youth culture the mantle of respectability is unfair and ill-advised. Prager goes on to remember, "Whole families would gather on Sunday evenings to listen to a half-hour radio program. Sandlot baseball and football were a way of life. As I grew older, the anticipation of a kiss after a movie date could be a kind of delirium. A dollar book, or better still a free one from the library, meant hours of pleasurable excitement. A Saturday afternoon movie was Heaven." The children of his generation did not need Alice Cooper.

Today, adults who are eager to endow their children with the innocence of youth and the profundity or wisdom of maturity are often shocked to find that their offspring possess neither. This does not mean that children cannot see through certain manifestations of hypocrisy or that teenagers or young adults cannot have personal identities. But often the confusion of the youth culture results from their very lack of background and exposure to life. At its worst, the new culture results in Alice Coopers, in sick, confused efforts to find new thrills or kicks, all in the name of idealism. At its best, the new culture represents confusion. A columnist once recalled his children's amazement when they discovered a "new sound" on a Beatle record. The sound, which they had never heard before, was a string quartet. Young people need to be guided and directed. They should be introduced to the best music, literature, theater, and art. Parents should remember that their children need to follow their examples.

They are seeking, searching, often trying to find themselves and establish a personal identity for their lives. Too often such considerations become exercises in the abstract. Young men and women are seeking "communication" or "their real selves." In truth they are seeking guidance and leadership out of the wilderness. The world is a confusing and complex place; there is no guarantee that specific members of the older generation can provide the guidance and leadership required. Obviously some cannot manage their own lives, let alone assist anyone else in clarifying his own values. But guidance and leadership (which may be expected in some degree of mature adults) will not be achieved if the men and women of American society plunge into a headlong flight toward middle-aged adolescence. How can adults deal with problems or challenges with insight and perception if they are devoting their time to copying, imitating, and approving any fashion, fad, or idea that is labeled "young," regardless of its intrinsic worth?

Donald Barr has counseled parents to provide alternatives for young persons. He says, "Parents must pass judgment with casual ruthlessness. The answer to " 'But Cheryl is allowed to! ' is 'Our family has higher standards than Cheryl's family.' "

He also urges parents to find manageable risks for their children, i.e., sailing, mountain-climbing, skiing, football, etc., when appropriate. The needs to achieve, to accomplish, to prove one's courage are very real.

Parents cannot just be "against" drugs; they must be "for" a way of life which does not require dependence on artificial kicks or chemically induced escapes. If a parent cannot think of valid alternatives to drugs, he has a problem and should re-examine his own priorities. Similarly, intelligent criticism of insipid rock music or obscenity in underground newspapers is not enough. Professors must be prepared to demonstrate the artistic and cultural worth of the great masterpieces of Western civilization. (Reciting some monotonous facts or declaring that Beethoven was a genius is begging the question.) Adults must recognize that cultural commodities patronized by young adults are not in themselves progressive or constructive, merely because of their origins.

Parents who devote their lives exclusively to material profit cannot offer regimented pursuit of "success" as an alternative to the dubious joys of unwashed hippiedom. Men and women who regard their own moral standards as conveniently adjustable to their pragmatic desires cannot offer "idealized" morality as an alternative to their own hypocrisy. Men and women are human; they are not saints. But society often revels in hypocrisy. Charles Reich and the other apologists can recognize some of this hypocrisy. But they cannot recognize the utter amorality and cultural sterility of their own alternatives. The professor, the parent, or the mature adult who says, "Me too" has no alternatives. He has only a vacuum, and is in many ways as confused and insecure as the young men and women whose behavior he seeks to emulate.

VII.

THE QUEST FOR IDENTITY

We take our colors, chameleon-like, from each other . . . .
Sebastian Roch Chamfort

Most people are other people. Their thoughts are someone else's opinions, their lives a mimicry, their passions a quotation . . . .
Oscar Wilde

In the 1960's, one after another of our traditional institutions was challenged. For a while, "dropping out" seemed fashionable. Now, in the 1970's, with the passing of the hippies as a major social element, psychologists and sociologists are borrowing ideas and behavioral patterns from the counterculture. Gradually, the dress, music, books, speech patterns, manners (or lack of them), and ideas of the counterculture are offered to society as new influences on the cultural mainstream. These negative solutions to problems were not a panacea to the dropouts; when applied to family life or to the lives of those who have decided to drop back in, the result is predictable: a blueprint for disaster.

We may easily recognize that a "meritocracy" may possess some drawbacks. In various roles or professions, the nature of "merit" may be determined by organizations or individuals who have acquired influence in a given field. The youth cult is outraged by the implication that "merit" is normally applied only in its functional sense, rather than in ways which are "aesthetically meaningful" to those who wish to turn society inside-out.

Unfortunately, society possesses no alternative to this perspective. If "merit," regardless of its definition, is not applied as a means for distinguishing between men, what other standard is equally valid? The assumption that financially remunerative professions mean that persons thereby engaged are "better" or "superior" than persons engaged in activities which provide little financial reward is unfortunate. Such attitudes will persist as long as man continues to evaluate other men in materialistic terms. If the popularly held notion that a lawyer is more "successful" than a bricklayer is undesirable, the condition will not improve because a third party intervenes with the intent of establishing financial parity between lawyers and bricklayers.

In the event that attempts at financial leveling are undertaken by the state, the ultimate result will not be the upgrading of bricklayers, but the downgrading of lawyers. Concurrently, the establishment of such "equality" is in fact the blatant sanction of *inequality*, and a significant step toward Big Brother.

To recognize that the highly specialized services of some physicians or attorneys are less easily obtained in society than the services of manual laborers is merely to acknowledge the demands of the marketplace. Efforts to control such demands have been historically disastrous.

In academic circumstances, teachers find it necessary to depend on a variety of grading procedures in evaluating students.

Initially, a prime function of "grading" was to inform the student of the nature of his work. In a teacher-pupil relationship, meaningful progress cannot be achieved if the pupil is presumed to know more about the subject studied than the instructor. In practice, grading has often degenerated into an artificial teaching tool that enables incompetent instructors to threaten or abuse students who do not share their beliefs. (This reference is primarily to forms of higher education. If a sixth grader chooses to believe that fractions are irrelevant to making change, or a fourth grader decides that 2+2=5, we cannot speak of differences of opinion.)

Too often a grade becomes an artificial symbol; the student must pursue the grade, not the knowledge. In turn, the grade may be achieved by compliance with standards or techniques which are essentially unrelated to the discipline as a whole. Testing or examination procedures may be abusive or unfair. Multiple-choice tests present classic examples of a test form which, when applied arbitrarily, may penalize the thinking student in favor of his less imaginative colleagues.

But again, reason must prevail. Even if educators freely concede that grading and testing procedures need careful re-examination, such changes must be approached from the standpoint of reform if the system of education is to survive. If examinations for drivers who seek applications fail to eliminate all unsafe drivers, we should not therefore abolish the procedure of driver-testing.

Intelligent criticism may be directed at a variety of teaching techniques and procedures as means of evaluating student performance. But efforts to abolish "merit" as a *sine qua non* consideration in student-teacher relationships is to go far beyond the boundaries of intelligent criticism.

If a teacher or principal cannot set standards for merit, who should? Certainly, students themselves are not in a position to set such standards for their own self-interest precludes objectivity. Advocates of "student power" are willing to assume the corruptibility of private corporations and the inefficiency of the regulatory agencies responsible for overseeing their activities.

Why then must we fail to challenge the peculiar notion that the perfectibility of man is applicable to high-school students but not corporation executives? Are teenagers more qualified to evaluate their own work than businessmen?

An unfortunate corollary in such discussions often interferes with an intelligent solution. Objections to the abolition of a "meritocracy" are dismissed as stubborn, unfeeling resistance to the inevitability of change. If specifics are examined, however, we easily see how the misinterpretation of faculty authority may be a stimulus to academic deterioration.

Students are often inclined to assume that their present tastes in books, films, music, and art are more *relevant* to their futures than time spent acquiring a familiarity with the cogent ideas and significant achievements of former times. A negative view of tradition is often encouraged by middle-aged professors nervously trying to identify with contemporary trends, thus preserving their own claims to professional esteem. Equation of "newness" with relevance is distinctly ill-advised. Wiley Housewright, former President of Music Educators' National Conference, urged that public schools begin immediately introducing rock music into their curricula. A basis for this proposition was Housewright's assumption that the music which was most familiar to young people would be a valuable teaching aid in "communicating" with them. Similar arguments could be advanced in behalf of such dubiously non-academic publications as comic books, *Mad* magazine, baseball cards, motion picture gossip magazines, and other items of interest to children. If a majority of sixth graders were invited to choose between spending an hour learning to read or watching television, the children might instinctively select the latter, even though the former would be infinitely more "relevant" to their education.

Similarly, ice cream cones are more "relevant" than spinach. Wiley Housewright was oblivious to the nature of teaching when he decided to jump on the bandwagon of teachers who feel that pop music communicates with children. If boys and girls are not already inundated to a point of saturation with commercially prepackaged pop culture, they will be when their "progressive" teachers are through with them.

Housewright assumed that because rock music exists, it is therefore "relevant." But the mere existence of any aspect, characteristic, or element in a culture does not in itself justify its inclusion in the curriculum. To suggest that students' judgment and teachers' judgment are collectively "equal" is nonsense. A hallmark of befuddled thinking with reference to the curriculum has arisen during the last few years. A number of educators have taken to suggesting that all subjects not deemed "relevant" by high-school or college students should be eliminated entirely from the curriculum. A further suggestion implies that faculty members who have insisted on the validity of these subjects should feel guilty regarding their past indiscretion. Profound exercises in public guilt are fashionable among apologists for the youth cult, who seem to regard a public confession of past aberrations in the name of tradition as an initiation exercise in progressive thought.

College catalogues are full of courses that are indeed irrelevant, unnecessary, and useless. The professor who turns his class over to an assistant, who drones and mumbles his fifteen-year-old lecture notes, and then assigns a devastating "grade" to his pupils, based on a single terrifying examination, is helping no one. But if the narrow-minded, trivia-seeking, incompetent bureaucrat is a vestigial participant in today's academic world, so is the self-appointed, egocentric, ignorant youth who regards his own immature whims as a suitable curriculum for himself and everyone else.

If a student were to propose, for example, that administrators develop a program designed to provide practical experience for students in their chosen fields, such a program might contain detailed proposals intended to offer students an improved opportunity to acquire some degree of expertise in their selected areas of endeavor. The academic world is ripe for reform. But the equation of each utterance by any spoiled brat who chooses to open his mouth with intelligent, constructive suggestions by students is to invite disaster. Teachers must retain the authority to set standards and develop goals. A school in which "merit" is to be declared meaningless is a school for morons.

Similarly, teachers are individuals. They have different tastes, theories, and attitudes. A school is a microcosm of a more complex society. Student protest was advertised as an outcry against the "lawless" authority exercised by the educators, because the corporate state (i.e., society) rewards those who complete school successfully. (No one bothered to ask which students were protesting or whether other students agreed.) Flexible curricula are desirable and essential if our educational institutions are to survive the ideological onslaught of anarchists who seek to subvert the schools to serve their own ends. But some negativists assail *all* authority because some has been abused.

It is one thing to recognize the mechanized, bureaucratic injustices that exist in the academy. It is quite another to assail the idea of "merit" as a form of precipitating inequality. The most insipid criticism conceivable suggests that schools are engaged in a vast program of indoctrination designed to prepare persons for predetermined roles in an artificial society. Such characterization implies a machine of overpowering efficiency. In truth, the schools are often inefficient. Their greatest difficulty is not their diabolical cunning, but their slow, complex ways of achieving constructive change, coupled with an overpowering inefficiency and lack of direction. Administrators often demonstrate an incapacity to distinguish between growth and progress, or between expansion and improvement. We may well desire a re-examination of our definition of merit; we cannot afford the glorification of academic deterioration in the name of student-teacher equality.

Amid the confusion that prevades our society, recent trends in sociological analysis have encouraged an emphasis on expression of the "real self". Invariably, the "real self" is characterized as "honest," "unaffected," and "natural." In contrast to the qualities which the counterculture defines as manifestations of "uptightness," fear, rigidity, and an outer veneer of reserve concealing an inner self riddled with frustrations, the new "self" is portrayed as ideal.

Men and women who have discovered their "true identities" are described as relaxed, sensitive, and eager to engage in personal relationships. Artificiality and tolerance for pressures have allegedly dissapeared. The social restrictions imposed by concerns for competence have vanished too. Instead, we have man in his "natural" state, free of neuroses and tensions, ready to love his fellow human beings and engage in the most meritorious forms of self-expression. Certainly, this is a highly desirable picture. But these are generalities. How are these wonderful qualities to be recognized in more specific contexts? To a sociological theoretician, being specific is to be avoided at all costs.

As an example of "uptightness," Charles Reich invites us to consider the housewives, "looking out from their windows, as if spying an unexpected patch of dirt in an otherwise spick and span house." Efforts by the police or by persons who may be characterized as "solid citizens" to identify strangers in the neighborhood who seem "different" are ridiculed as examples of "managerial paranoia."

To discern the illogic in such attitudes, we must remember that nature contains many elements which are undesirable. Some animals may be friendly to man, but thoroughly hostile to other animals. The mere "existence" of any element in nature does not justify its inclusion in a list of "desirables" for society. A skunk, for instance, is "real." It exists. It belongs to nature. We assume, too, that the skunk is "honest." Even the most rabid apologists for the youth cult would find it difficult to welcome the aroma of a skunk as a "desirable" for society. But when hundreds of young people abstain from bathing or grooming, their acquisition of their own odoriferous aroma suddenly becomes a holy crusade, a means of "liberation." In reality, these persons are being "freed" from cleanliness, and "liberated" enough to achieve a familiarity with filth. Body odor becomes "escape from artifice." Through this neat, tidy semantic sleight of hand, apologists for the new youth culture are able to make persons who bathe appear to be stodgy, frustrated, and thoroughly enslaved by the "system" or the Establishment.

Similarly, social graces become topics of amusement. The distinctions between refinement and vulgarity are obliterated. Perons who have discovered the "new self" are eager to hasten their demise. Instead, a new, imprecise, inarticulate means of expression is proposed. Deviations are not permitted. Persons who do not immediately conform to the new conversational fads are subjected to ridicule.

Young people (and their middle-aged imitators) who speak in such terminology speak of "being where its at," "grooving," "rapping," "splitting," "living at one's pad," becoming "what's happening," avoiding persons who are "uptight." The more obvious teenage examples are readily punctuated with interjections of "like this" or "like that"; sentences are interrupted constantly with "man" or "you know." Reduction of the English language to its lowest common denominator is not a discovery of teenagers. Tarzan managed to make himself understood when he said, "Me — Tarzan, You — Jane." One father managed to respond to his son's assertion, "I have to find the real me," with the suggestion, "Why don't you try looking under your hair? " A facetious answer to be sure, and one that will be denounced by the youth cult as hostile and "uptight." Such an assertion merely indicates the grim, humorless attitude that pervades the cult's adherents.

Not only is the new "vocabulary" widespread, its advocates regard its application, along with an appreciation of rock music, drugs, and long hair, as an inviolate component of a new set of mores and folkways. Woe to the young man or woman who is articulate, verbally or grammatically. Faculty psychologists will be quick to recognize that the ability to express one's self beyond the most primitive linguistic level is a manifestation of "uptightness," maladjustment, and a failure to identify with one's peer group. In other words; like, man, baby — good grammar — we'd better split and go to our pad and rap in our own way. Doing our thing is where it's at and if we want to be what's happening, it ain't grooving to use good English.

Having disposed of personal cleanliness and the English language as minor casualties, the youth cult was ready to consume bigger and better rivals. Next on the agenda was a "redefinition" or "reconstitution" of some basic moral attitudes that seem to be constantly impeding the inevitability of youthful "progress." Despite the self-righteous concern for "human relationships" which are part of the new youth culture, one of the essential elements of the "new self" is the "redefinition" of "love." Motion pictures and television, eager to capitalize on the sensationalism resulting from such considerations, assisted in burying the old institution of romance as fast as they could find a dirty shovel.

It is easy to sneer at "romance." Attitudes regarding what is or is not romantic during a specific era may change. But the youth cult prides itself on its ability to "love." But the latter, as defined by the broadcast media and film industry, is principally a hurried effort to demonstrate how boy meets girl and the two of them rush off to the bedroom to "do their thing." The slogan, "Make love, not war" suddenly becomes "Make sex, not war." Implicit in this original slogan was the concept that "love" (i.e., relationships based on affection, mutual respect, and commitment) was preferable to war (killing of other human beings). But when the slogan is used by apologists for the youth cult, the meaning of "Make love, not war" is clear: indulge your whims. Publicity notices for a commercially exploited play that contains considerable emphasis on nudity, declared that the production concerned 'dirty" things like napalm and "clean" things like nudity and lovemaking. The producer and writers expect the audience to read a deeply profound message into this material. But the suggestion of fast, non-committal, superficial biological relationships, is anything but a suggestion of "love." Promiscuity thus becomes alternative to napalm. Why should intelligent men accept the proposition that one necessarily justifies, or is even related to, the other? The show was named appropriately, *The Dirtiest Show in Town*.

In films, free and explicit sex have become symbolic of "honesty." "Love" is reduced to those occurrences which may appear in a biology textbook. Like the dirty young man who regards his slovenly appearance as a means of "liberation," the free love advocates succeed only in clouding the issue. In their world, promiscuity becomes a virtue. Constancy becomes a vice. Apologists for the youth culture engage in clever "redefinitions," and "love," like the English language is reduced to its lowest common denominator.

We may also observe that those who trumpet the "sexual revolution" may be self-seeking in their motives. Charles Reich is eager to remind us that among the "freedoms" denied us by the corporate state are "sex exchanged between two couples, communal sex, homosexuality, and polymorphous sexual expression."

Adultery, of course, is the most basic freedom "denied us." Curiously enough, theoreticians who advocate the "new morality" can remember the "thou shalt not" aspects of killing, but not of adultery. It appears that knowledge of the Bible, like knowledge of everything else in the youth cult, is generally confined to a distinct selectivity.

The motion-picture industry and theater have become institutions for expressions of such viewpoints. Significantly, William Goldman observed in his startling book *The Season*, that possibly one third of Broadway's plays and musicals were produced, written, or directed by a large number of homosexuals. We should not be surprised that these men applaud the assertion in *The Greening of America*, that long-haired youths do not doubt their masculinity. These men don't doubt theirs either; they haven't for a long time. But are we naïve enough to believe that the enormous community of homosexuals, many of them articulate, quite talented, and extremely influential, who have kept their private lives a secret from the public, are objective on the subject?

The key to a "redefinition" of "love" (or anything else) is to persuade society that a condition previously regarded as undesirable is actually quite ordinary. (The assumption that ordinariness and desirability are synonymous is one of the classic rationalizations of the youth cult.) Once we are persuaded that the "new morality" has a claim to normalcy, non-adherents to the new attitudes are made to feel that they are abnormal, different, and somehow wrong. The very techniques that induce conformity, abhorred by the youth cult on a superficial level, are thus used to enforce compliance. In reality, the youth cult does not find conformity distasteful, but rather conformity to ideas which are not deemed popular by self-styled arbiters of youthful taste.

By this curious indulgence in *non sequitur*, a runaway hippie girl who is willing to "love" a different boy every week suddenly becomes a "living protest against war." Prostitution has always thrived during wartime. While the girl may choose to delude herself that she is "better" than the prostitute (a pernicious retrogression to status seeking which

Reich would undoubtedly deplore), her bahavior, for admittedly different reasons, may be essentially the same.

Curiously, four-letter words which relate to biological
functions become further manifestations of "honesty." The
youth cult loves to sneer and smirk over the use of euphe-
misms by those whose "Victorian morality" renders them
impervious to the appeals of underground newspapers. They
do not recognize the inconsistency of their assertion, on one
hand, that "love" is man's highest function, and their dependence, on the other hand, on a code of social behavior
that describes man's "natural" functions in the basest ways
imaginable. Too often, our literature and motion pictures
reflect an assumption that the most bizarre and abnormal
practices of man are quite normal. We are advised that perversion is not really objectionable, so long as it constantly
reflects good taste. Persons making such assertions do not
recognize that perversions and immorality represent the
antithesis of good taste; they are mutually exclusive.

The classic example of such misunderstanding is the
assumption that any "natural function of man" is therefore
appropriate at any place or time. (Again, we see the redefinition principle at work, the student who defecates in the
student union reception room at Berkeley suddenly establishes a "union with nature," because he is exercising a
natural function of man. Ecology is thus brought into play,
and like a superpatriot wrapping himself in the flag, the
unwashed rebel justifies his own perverse behavior by identi-
fying it with some laudable causes which are totally unrelated.)

If we return for a moment to the scene of suburban
tranquility misinterpreted by many, we can see how the
techniques of "redefinition" can be used to examine a situation, turn it inside-out and upside-down, and ultimately
persuade us that, like the audience at a magic show, we
haven't seen what we've really seen at all.

The housewife is characterized as suspicious, insensitive,
and afraid. Police officers are described as apprehensive and
ready to assume the worst, regarding strangers. The police
may be seen "investigating" those who appear "different" in

the nice, clean, immaculate suburb. Finally, "solid citizens" of the suburb, men amd women who are familiar with each other's ideas and personalities, reveal their prejudices and fears. In the dropout's perspective, and employing his terminology, everyone is "uptight."

If we examine the suburb more closely, however, we can see a very different picture from the one often presented to us. The housewife may work long hours in the garden, tending her flowers and planting new ones. She may have children who play on the front lawn or go around the block to join other boys and girls in the neighborhood. The same can be said for the "solid citizens" who work, pay taxes, possess a normal number of human virtues and faults, and go about their business. Into the suburb comes a young man with hair down to his shoulders. He is easily identified by an odoriferous aura; he is unkempt, unwashed, and dirty. When greeted by the townspeople, he is rude, discourteous, and quick to use obscene language. If persons try to make friendly conversation with him, he responds with a series of grunts or noises which are supposed to provide some special meaning. Why is the housewife concerned about him? First of all, he may choose to trample her flowers or defecate on her lawn. (At Berkeley, students, like dogs, learn to "do their own thing" when the impulse strikes.) He may introduce her children to obscene language or worse, to a variety of dangerous drugs. He may be addicted to drugs himself, and therfore inclined to a variety of crimes in order to support his habit. He may decide to wander around town in the nude, thus subjecting a majority of the townspeople to what *they* consider to be an indignity. (Whether this young man considers it is an indignity, or we do, for that matter, is irrelevant.) It is *their* town because they live there, work there, and are entitled to maintain a sense of public decency if they so choose.

This does not mean that a drug pusher cannot wear a gray flannel suit. Some do. This does not suggest that a man wearing an Oriental robe and a long beard cannot be a philosopher. Many are. But in turn, critics are in no way justified in ridiculing the housewife because she wants her children safe, her lawn clean, and *her* rights protected. The police are always easy to abuse. Policemen normally meet men and women at the unhappiest times of their lives. Law violators are not happy to see policemen. Officers are human; they are not gods (or devils); they cannot make claims to either perfection or universal corruptibility. They are just men, trying to do their job, a job which is dangerous and difficult.

Police officers are abused, threatened, ridiculed, cursed, and subjected to a variety of physically intimidating attitudes. During the course of a day, a policeman may have to face rocks, bottles, physical assaults, and bullets. When the policemen are "cruising around the suburb," what are they trying to accomplish? They are obviously not trying to become wealthy. If they were, they wouldn't be on the police force. One function of the police is to protect the rights of citizens.

If the police themselves are unnecessarily violent in dealing with a suspect, they are engaged in wrongdoing themselves. Considering the pressures to which policemen are subjected today, we may well concede a human tendency toward overreaction. But to describe every incident involving a policeman's gun as "police brutality" or every episode in which an officer uses force to subdue a suspect as "authoritarian repression" is a disservice to the entire concept of law enforcement. Citizens would do well to remember that a man caught robbing a bank is not about to surrender to officers because the policeman walks up to him and says, "Like baby, let's split to the police pad and arrest you."

The most insidious implication of the unwashed conformists is their assertion that the police, by their very diligence in perusing the activities of a peculiar looking stranger in the community, are somehow engaged in wrongdoing. We are never told by anyone why this police action should be objectionable. But by innuendo amd implication, we are urged to believe that such police behavior is an integral part of the massive conspiracy of the Establishment to restrict us.

In this upside-down, inside-out, never-never land, our values suddenly reverse. At America's Mad Tea Party, we are told glowingly of the toleration of young people for each other, a reverence for one's "freaky friends." In this world, it is desirable, even laudatory, to be freaky; it is reprehensible to be clean or solid. Again, redefinition procedures seek to persuade us that our natural concerns for our safety, morals, well-being, and survival are in some way "unnatural." Rising crime rates are common knowledge. Residents of the suburbs, like the cities, fear murder, robbery, rape, burglary, drug addiction, and overall moral erosion. Because we hear about so much crime, we tend to accept it as "normal." During the 1920's, the Loeb-Lepopold case provoked an outcry from citizens everywhere. Public outrage was militant and widespread. Today, such a case might receive some publicity; but unless a crime achieves ghoulish proportions or involves a famous public figure, notices of crime are taken matter of factly.

The youth culture has done nothing to divorce itself from crime. While superficially advertising itself as a culture based upon the innocence of children, the new life-styles of some youths have lent themselves easily to the encouragement of crime. One need only examine the statistics of crime in the Haight-Ashbury district of San Francisco (or the lawless bahavior of Berkeley students and street people) to recognize this fact. The Students for a Democratic Society have often received police protection for their marches. In Chicago, they broke away from such protection and went on a rampage with bricks, chains, and clubs. At Stanford University and Columbia University, violence led to the destruction of valuable research papers and library materials belonging to distinguished scholars.

Again we must reiterate that a community is not assuming that anyone with long hair has arrived in town to set fire to the local library or throw rocks at nearby windows. But those men and women who are aware that the youth culture, as a whole, has an execrable record regarding crime, are merely apprehensive and they should be. The egregious troublemakers and inveterate liars have created a distaste in the minds of many that carries over to affect a basic perspective of young people. Apologists should remember that the youth culture has created its own poor image; it is merely reaping the results of its ill-sown seeds.

If a group of young men and women want to move into a community and tread upon the rights of others, they may choose to disregard the egocentricity of their actions. But if the community, through its leaders, citizens, police, and elected officials, chooses to respond by inviting the young men and women to leave, the community is within its rights. In Carmel, California, a small army of hippies managed to turn a pastoral hamlet into a place where dirty vagabonds were to be seen on every street corner. The community had to place locks on all the public restrooms in town. Dogs accompanied the hippies, along with their natural involvement in the drug mystique. No community should be required to tolerate filth, drug addiction, or the indulgence of parasitic youths who expect society (i.e., the Establishment) to provide their food, shelter, and indulgence of their whims.

When citizens in Carmel responded with an efficacious program to get rid of the hippies, the hue and cry was immediately raised. Carmel residents obviously didn't understand "what the kids want."

Perhaps in a world of Mad Hatters and March Hares, sensibility and sanity may seem out of place. But in our society, we court disaster if we redefine our terms in such a way as to reverse our values. George Orwell suggested in *1984* the ultimate adoption of "newspeak," a modern terminology which would supersede real language in the totalitarian state. We don't have to wait for 1984; "open-minded reformers" are urging us, "Move right on," always, of course, in the name of progress.

The new "honesty" is, in fact, a sham. It is a foolish myth designed to persuade sane men that they are mad. In a recent Broadway play, *Butterflies are Free*, an East Village director, one of the characters in the plot, is enthusiastically promoting the "new honesty." He rattles off a long list of sordid and distasteful activities which occur in society. When he finishes, he declares to the central figure, a middle-aged lady from the suburbs, "You can't object to these. They occur as part of real life! " She responds curtly, "So does diarrhea, but I don't want to see it on the stage." Nor anywhere else, we may well add!

The "new honesty" emerges as an old artifice. Suddenly, we are presented with a new, sacrosanct youth culture. If we recognize its weakness, we deserve better than childish abuse.

VIII.

THE YOUTH CULTURE:
EVOLUTION IN REVERSE

A bad man is worse when he pretends to be a saint .. Francis Bacon

The devil can cite Scripture for his purpose. An evil soul, producing holy witness, is like a villain with a smiling cheek; a goodly apple rotten at the heart. .... William Shakespeare

At the very heart of the youth culture, we find a confident self-assertion of righteousness. In many ways, this attitude is similar to the most rigid and restrictive viewpoints inherent in conservative religions of former times. The Puritans, we are told, took a dim view of man's pursuit of pleasure, with special emphasis on sex. The youth cult, however, reverses this stand. Everyone "must" believe in the complete moral justification of each man to pursue his whims on all matters, concerning sex or anything else. Everyone "must" approve or acknowledge the validity of anyone else's bahavior. To express even the remotest doubts regarding a man's morals, his character, or the way he chooses to lead his life, is indicative of "Puritanical tendencies" or worse, "a capacity to judge others." Thus, the youth cult thrives on an artificial arbitrary, and capricious assumption: society is expected to abolish all considerations of taste or morality in the name of "equality." Apologists for the youth cult fail to realize that their efforts to create a society in which there are no restrictions merely encourage a new form of acquiescence. Suddenly, we are faced with an inverse Puritan ethic, which requires, immediately, that we countenance all forms of sexual behavior. Dissenters are instantly labeled "Establishment," "old-fashioned," "Puritanical," or "irrelevant." A variety of derisive terms are available.

In this upside-down, inside-out world, "restrictions" are identified with "expression." The two terms are obviously not synonymous. Therefore, society is expected to yield to small groups of persons who desire no restrictions. Society, however, cannot function in a vacuum. If we abandon all private rules and guidelines for behavior, we are, in effect, enforcing the tastes and preferences of those who seek to establish an anarchistic state. Violence by high-school and college students has often been rationalized, because apologists offer the excuse that violence is perpetrated against the students themselves. Some academicians have gone so far as to suggest that violence is any assault upon the personality. Thus, the student can redefine requirements that he carry a pass to walk in the hall or attend public school until he is sixteen as a form of "violence," and respond by vandalizing the school.

Herein lies the most pernicious aspect of the youth cult: its inability to distinguish between extremes. Certainly, requirements for hall passes may be offensive to some high-school students. For openers, they offend persons intent upon cutting classes, for a variety of reasons. In most schools, education is supposed to be taking place in the classrooms, not in the halls. If a student wants to walk around in the halls, he should have a good reason. Junior-high-school boys and girls are fond of smoking, and activity that is difficult to pursue in the midst of a history lesson. High-school periods are usually brief, forty-five minutes to an hour. Teachers have enough problems today without encountering an additional one: the "right" of any "student" to wander around aimlessly in the halls, to gossip with friends about the latest favorite among local disc jockeys, to smoke, drink, or leave the school grounds at will during class time. Schools accept responsibility for minors when they

open their doors to children of a community. The local principal cannot assume responsibility for the behavior of
persons who may be waiting outside the school grounds
seeking to "communicate" with students. In today's complex
society, a student may find narcotics peddlers prowling
around the fence, that would serve to illustrate the false
theory of "repression." He may also find a variety of young
adults who are taking time away from their usual activity,
tearing up the local college campus, to pay him a visit. These
persons are eager to introduce him to the joys of the unwashed revolution, if he has by some chance failed to discover them for himself. Perhaps a high-school boy's intentions outside of the classroom are not sinister at all: he may
want to go across the street for a hamburger, or to visit his
girl friend in another building. Rules regarding hall passes
were established to prevent activities which most schools
regard as undesirable and detrimental to the process of education.

Many "progressive" citizens are inclined to assume the
innate beneficence of high-school students, characterized,
naturally, as "the kids." We have no reason to assume that
Johnny or Mary are paragons of moral virtue because they
are teenagers. When critics talk about the "violence" of the
high-school, they fail to mention the violent and intimidating
atmosphere encountered by teachers. Many instructors in
urban areas have discovered to their horror that *The Black-
board Jungle* is more than the title of a successful motion
picture or novel.

Society has always functioned on the assumption that
men who are civilized condemn violence. Not all men are
civilized, even at this late date. Our daily newspapers are
quick to remind us that violence functions regularly, to the
detriment of society in general. Suddenly, however, "violence" has been redefined. Hall passes and other forms of
regulation are now "violent," just as violent as the forms of
physical or emotional abuse we read about in the papers.
(The student who protests against hall passes is expressing
his outrage against war, racism, totalitarianism, and repression.) The sixteen-year-old boy who wants to smoke or drink

in the restroom is presented to us as a political martyr. If two teenage girls want to argue over the assertion that Mick Jagger's hair is longer than Frank Zappa's, their English teacher's insistence that they concentrate on a definition of adverbs, is a manifestation of "repression" (i.e., a form of violence).

Other regulations or precedents which displease high-school boys and girls are denounced as assaults upon the self. Ultimately, this nonsense leads to the sanctity of disorder. Social observers beg the question when they make excuses about students being provoked to violence. If high-school students interpret their spelling assignments as "violence," but the students want to respond by burning all the spelling books in the school, these sympathetic adults want to invite someone else to accept the blame.

There is no denying that high-schools are overcrowded and often understaffed. We cannot seriously challenge the assertion that methods of education can always be improved. We may well object to grading procedures, not because they imply "judgment," but because they provide the teacher and the pupil with an artificial goal, a symbol which often becomes more important than the process of education itself. But if we try to abolish judgment we shall fail. If each student's behavior is declared, legally, to be "equal" to every other student's behavior, with no rules, grades, standards, or qualifications, we are committing the worst judgment of all. We are engaged in the process of leveling, an artificial means of equalizing which negates, among other things, the capacity of a school to function.

In discussing the student-teacher relationship, too many students and teachers alike have assumed, by definition, that students possess the virtues of Pollyanna, while principals, teachers, or other authority figures are portrayed as having the same sensitivity we would expect in a representative of the Spanish Inquisition. Students can be troublemakers; if they are trying to initiate a revolution and replace the senior prom with a workshop on guerrilla warfare, they are inviting an authoritative (and hopefully, effective) response.

The equation of rules, grades, and an unequal student-teacher relationship with violence does a disservice to education. A non-violent society, one in which no forms of violence would be necessary, might be an idyllic utopia. But to equate sincere opposition to real violence with whimsical resistance to all forms of legitimate authority is a corruption of the word.

Ultimately, the youth cult claims to restore those aspects of the human experience which have been lost through adherence to roles, fostering of a meritocracy, and acceptance of the work ethic. Adoption of the new life-styles is supposed to represent the panacea, the solution, the cure-all which can help us to regain the lost self.

The primary purpose of these lost elements is to confuse the issue. It is easier to persuade sane men to speak out in favor of ecology, than to turn the discussion of the People's Park into a consideration of the street people and their plans to promote a municipal brand of Marxism. It is easier to talk about artistic creativity than to dwell upon the inarticulate new writers whose philosophical profundity cannot go beyond "do your own thing." It is easier to talk about freedom than to justify the bad taste which is worn as a badge of distinction by the unwashed, foul-mouthed rabble-rousers and their neater, but terribly confused academic admirers.

By linking the counterculture with high ideals, through skillful redefinitions, psychologists and social observers can persuade us that the changes taking place in our country are perfectly normal, very much in fashion, and not worth a moment of concern. They provide the youth cult with some respectability it has been unable to acquire as a result of its own intrinsic merit. Consider some of the ways in which society is being changed today. A host of journalists and sociological speculators are applauding these changes with glee. But when the evidence is considered, we quickly see the error of their ways. Society should have regarded the youth cult for what it was: a Mad Tea Party, a costume ball, a bizarre sideshow, a cultural aberration. Instead, middle class and upper class values have been readjusted to integrate the influences of the youth cult in our social mainstream.

The cultural revolution: Participation in artistic endeavor is a noteworthy activity of which men may be proud. The explosion of creative activities on the part of young people, especially in musical and cinematic projects, is often presented as a means of proving that "the kids are all right after all." Concurrently, the adults who do not subscribe to the youth cult, those who are offended by the underground poetry in the high-school papers, the unkempt rock groups, the pseudo-pornographic films, are subjected to ridicule. They are obviously square: they are inartistic; they only understand the process of making money. But the youth cult has actively downgraded the artistic achievements of most of Western civilization. The rock-group leader who knows four chords or the creator of nonsense poetry or the avantgarde painter who takes aim at his canvas and lets the paint fall where it will are prime examples. These persons all demand the respect (and even the patronage) of society because of their inflated impressions of their own talents. But the critics and journalists who applaud these cultural advances dismiss most of the great works of art in Western civilization. Their rationale is justified by their assumption that the only relevant works of art today are those which reinforce the social or political complaints of the counterculture.

A typical example of the new culture is a poem by R. Crumb, creator of numerous underground comic books, who suggests an ideal world: a society in which every one from Peter Pan to the Pope would be "stoned," on trips induced by psychedelic drugs. Presumably the composers or writers who do not adhere to the basic doctrines of the counterculture, whose every work is not steeped in anti-Establishment propaganda, are to be dismissed. This attitude is not dissimilar to the state control over the arts that exists in the Soviet Union, where distinguished creators have been taken to task because their works do not reflect the current taste of the bureaucracy in books or music.

Advocates of the youth cult are concerned with the ability to listen to others. This is utter nonsense. Apologists for the self-styled "now" generation are constantly talking about the lack of communication. They insist that the new etiquette, the informal dress and manners, the new standards of taste, and attention to what the kids want, will establish greater communication between the generations.

They do not practice what they preach. They have demonstrated no desire whatsoever to "listen" to the views of young people who do not wear bell bottoms, beards, or long hair. Did the students of Berkeley or Columbia express an interest in listening when they turned to wanton destruction of private property, when mobs attempted to shout down faculty members who did not subscribe to their political views? No evidence has been presented to indicate that marriage, a career, or traditional moral values are mutually exclusive with meaningful, personal relationships.

If a man fosters artificial relationships, and he happens to earn a monthly salary in a specific job, nothing restrains him from re-evaluating his goals or his ideas. The youth cult thrives on the assumption that substitution of casual relationships for a marriage contract makes the relationships more "meaningful." Pursuing aimless searching instead of a career makes the former "thoughtful."

Perhaps a man has discovered what he likes to do best in the world, and wishes to pursue that career to support his family. If a man is devoted to his wife, his family, and to pursuing goals that are non-materialistic, he can achieve all of these relationships within the system. Those persons who want to abolish our institutions imply that they are no longer useful and should be discarded. This is a classic case of *non sequitur*.

Expression of the individual self through dress. Parents and teachers who favor the imposition of dress codes are constantly reminded that "today's kids are informal," that "rules of dress don't matter to them." Yet some social critics have attempted to insist that the bizarre, slovenly dress standards adopted by many young people encourage fun, work, and dignity. Dignity has never mattered to the youth cult. Nude bathing, casual free love, and perpetual existence in the unwashed state hardly encouraged dignity. Non-adherents to the youth cult have lost the capacity to dress constantly in the most primitive state available to man.

It has become fashionable to ridicule middle-aged men and women who are offended by the filth and squalor that seems to pervade the existences of the Harvard student body as much as the hippies who disappeared as fast as they left then mark on the American way of life. Different forms of dress on different occasions are denounced as a manifestation of artifice.

In other words, a man who chooses to wear the same clothing all the time is "free." Bathing suits in church become appropriate. Some advocates of the counterculture have even suggested that there is a sociological sanctity about the right to always appear bare-footed in public. We may safely conclude that Western civilization will survive, even if a majority of the populace continues to wear shoes.

The spirit of universal brotherhood. We are told that man has lost the ability to be affectionate, to care about his fellow man, to believe in brotherhood. Even if we accept these assertions as true, does our answer lie with the counterculture? Yet many American families who remain within our social mainstream are borrowing from the counterculture and emulating its exponents. The "progressive" social analysts imply that the best way to regain our values is to either emulate the youth cult, or join it. During the 1960's, news reports often seemed to indicate that dropping out was the fashion. Now the trend has changed; in the 1970's, families seem to be adopting some of the tenets of the counterculture, even as the latter fades into historical oblivion.

Drugs, for instance, dominated the hippie society of the 1960's. Today, the drug problem is significant as a major menace to our school systems. Permanent commitments to a single individual, through marriage, assumption of responsibilities relating to the family or one's career, and respect for the rights of others are all avoided by proponents of the new morality. In what ways do adherents of the new youth culture express the aforementioned qualities? Certainly not by their disregard for other people's property, tastes, and values. Rock festivals policed by motorcycle gangs do not imply brotherhood. Violent demonstrations encouraged by doctrinaire Marxists do not imply tolerance.

The drug culture. We are urged to lament the fact that the oppressive Establishment has lost the opportunity to poison itself en masse through a plethora of drugs. The result has been fewer drug addicts, fewer suicides, and fewer persons ultimately facing the agony of withdrawal.

The new morality. Despite a surplus of glib literature immersed primarily in chic and fashionable psychological jargon, the new morality is built on an amoral view; it is inherently opposed to social morality of any type. When society expresses its own morality, through opposition to free love, nude bathing, rock festivals, dirt and filth spread by unwashed nomads, or regular dependence upon drugs by college students and a middle-aged élite, or other manifestations of the youth culture, society is subjected to vehement ridicule. The "new morality" has a neat rationale: whatever you want to do is moral, and if anyone questions you, blame it on the Establishment.

Proponents of the "new morality" cannot have it both ways. If they respect individual morality, they should cease and desist from mockery when groups of citizens express their concept of morality collectively. Such persiflage serves only to underscore the basic contempt of these social analysts for any "morality" which does not conform to popularly held notions of cult adherents and their middle-aged apologists. The morality of the youth cult is adjustable.

Many young persons choose to sneer at the Victorian morality of their elders while indulging in amoral behavior themselves. Destruction of private property, an immoral act, may be easily justified through semantic manipulations. Violence, also immoral, is similarly excused if such violence is perpetrated by adherents to the youth cult, as "defensive violence." The same rights of defense are not accorded to police or persons who are typecast as representative of the Establishment. Racism, another immoral element, is tolerated, if a manifestation of inverse racism. Persons identified with the Establishement may be ideal targets of inverse discrimination.

Respect for the law, respect for one's elders (not necessarily acquiescence but common courtesy), respect for the property and personal rights of others, are dismissed as irrelevant. Naturally, this is not the case if the rights in question are those of the New Left, the Now Generation, or any members of the élite prepared to remake society.

Morality is a two-way street. Too many young persons fall back on a holier-than-thou attitude when dealing with adults. The assertion "Never trust anyone over thirty" is itself discrimination, although the distinction is chronological rather than racial. We have no evidence that young persons or their middle-aged imitators are endowed with moral purity. The implication that persons who work for a living or dress conservatively are tools of the Establishment's corrupt morality is ridiculous. The age bias has been carried to its worst extreme on the high-school campuses, where student violence resulting in shootings and vandalism have become the order of the day. Laws against these activities relate to the over-thirty culture and the old morality; the "new morality" has already taken its toll.

Discussions about the "new morality" invariably turn to sex. It is a controversial subject, and it sells books or films or a variety of other products. We are told that the old morality is restrictive; instead, we can now enjoy the new freedom, which allows and encourages us to participate in a variety of sexual experiences with many different people. Fidelity is dismissed, replaced by a new casual approach which suits the whim. Critics of sex-education programs are often ridiculed and portrayed as prudish ladies in tennis shoes; but parents have cause for concern when they realize that instruction in sex-education classes may imply that morality (which is not discussed) has nothing to do with the subject. To omit discussion of prevailing moral views is to imply that these views are unimportant.

Personal fulfillment through achievement of one's own special excellence and worth. Efforts to encourage self-respect are praiseworthy. Too often, the youth cult substitutes self-satisfaction for self-respect. The result is predictable: the individual becomes smug and self-satisfied, encouraged by a society which declares (in the name of equality) that he cannot have faults or weaknesses which would render him unequal.

The concept of one's own special worth is used as an excuse to debunk excellence to encourage mediocrity. If a man wants to discover his own standard for "success," he is perfectly free to do so. If this man wants to pursue the career of a philosopher rather than that of an advertising executive, he may discover a personal definition of success. But that definition should not include an expectation that the world owes him a living, or that his creative efforts deserve to be encouraged by society simply because he thinks they are artistic and desirable.

Too often the youth cult has set itself up as an alternative to the work ethic, with the implication that those who work should be made to pay for the creative efforts of those who choose to devote their time to drugs, encounter groups, and the speeches of Jane Fonda.

Personal achievement is not highly regarded by those social observers who use the general welfare as an excuse to promote a welfare state.

The renaissance of emotion. The new youth cult is designed to perpetuate itself through a constant indulgence in man's finest emotions: bravery, courage, reverence, and romance. Yet the coarse, neurotic youth culture was built on disrespect for tradition, conformity, irreverence, and an assumption of infallibility. It is hardly capable of restoring these qualities.

The youth culture is the antithesis of romance. The art, music, and literature of the unwashed masses emphasizes realism. The underground press eschews refinement, taste, and respect. A culture which regards a four-letter obscenity as the best expression of one's feelings is hardly romantic, by anyone's definition.

Marriage, we are told, is an outdated institution; but it can be revitalized, they continue, through the use of a marriage contract, in which both parties agree to a complex legal arrangement; part of an arrangement is a statement of the rights and privileges of both persons, with special emphasis on the right of the wife to study karate or make speeches urging the abolition of men, or other appropriate activities for the liberated woman. If a married couple must engage in more complicated negotiations than the Paris Peace Talks in order to get married, the new marriage is a dubious institution. The marriage contract concept is an example of pseudo-intellectual efforts to accept the assertion of the counterculture during the 1960's (i.e., marriage is extinct) and to apply it to the 1970's. The difficulty arises from the fact that the youth cult of the 1960's was an aberration; marriage and the family must be revitalized, not destroyed or rendered inadequate.

Assumption of responsibilities is often unpleasant; the adult world is riddled with inconsistences, hypocrisies, and faults of all shapes and sizes. The search for the true self is complex; it cannot be ended by the assertion that a panacea for the human condition can best be realized through the adoption of dress, music, jargon, and complete capitulation to teenage whims. Grace and Fred M. Hechinger declared, in their book, *Teen-Age Tyranny*, "What worries us is not the greater freedom of today's youth, but rather the abdication of the rights and privileges of adults for the convenience of the immature. As a result, American society is growing down rather than growing up."

Before our search for the real self can be successful, we must assure ourselves that growth and attitudes progress in the right direction, not the wrong way.

IX.

BLUEPRINT FOR DISASTER:
THE YOUTH CULT REVOLUTION

Zeal is very blind, or badly regulated when it encroaches upon the rights of others . . . . Pasquier Quesnel

"Knowledge, without common sense", says Lee, "is folly; without method, it is waste; without kindness, it is fanaticism; without religion, it is death." But with common sense, it is wisdom; with method, it is power; with charity, it is beneficence; with religion, it is virtue, and life and peace . . . . Frederick William Farrar

When the term "revolution" is introduced into a conversation, most Americans picture a violent upheaval. We imagine a scene out of Dickens, with French nobles being marched off to the guillotine, and an eager Mme. DeFarge knitting furiously in the front row. When Americans think in terms of "revolutionaries," they often imagine sinister terrorist plots and clandestine meetings. Certainly revolutionaries of this sort do exist in contemporary society. But some theoreticians suggest that the youth cult represents a new form of social change, in which individuals change their own lives, and concurrently change society. In theory, at least, the idea seems to make sense. If enough individuals were to decide to become vegetarians, for example, the meat industry would have a problem. Meat packers do not concern themselves with this possible crisis, because they think that universal adoption of vegetarian ideas is highly unlikely.

At least for public consumption, the youth cult has advertised itself as non-violent, changing the political structure as its final act rather than as its initial *coup d'état*. Instead we are constantly reminded that the culture of "our young people" is a renaissance of the American spirit, a collective movement of individual acts which, when combined, will ultimately express the best ideals of the American dream. Such an assertion, while very desirable and optimistic, is easily proven to be superficial. The suggestion of a new renaissance of the American spirit implies that we have somehow gotten away from our heritage, our roots, our basic principles. If we believe what we are told, the lifestyles of certain young people — their taste in clothing, style, and manner, their use of drugs and dependance upon sex, their music, and ideological leanings toward collectivist philosophy — will lead us back to the things we have lost. But by definition, the youth culture is *against* perpetuation of a strong family unit, *against* traditional moral values, *against* most of the principles and ideals that have formed our social foundation. If the youth cult emerges triumphant, it will herald not the dynamic renewal of the American dream, but the beginning of its ultimate decline.

The self-styled cultural revolution known as the "counter-culture" has been based on certain assumptions. A brief examination of these assumptions reveals that they are shallow slogans with no real factual depth. Before examining the real meaning of the ways in which advocates of the new youth culture want to change our society, it is advisable to consider some of these myths.

The Establishment is hostile to the youth culture. Society is assumed to be innately suspicious of the quality of books, films, or music, which is steeped in the revolutionary doctrines of the counterculture. This is utter nonsense. To the contrary, society today makes things harder for those young people who do not subscribe to the counterculture. Middle-aged adolescents are usually quick to assume the inherent quality and "goodness" of music, art, or creative writings, if these works have been produced by members of the younger generation. The assumption equates "newness" with "pro-

gress." Because a motion picture or novel is recent, these
persons automatically endow its creator with "progressive"
qualities. They specifically discount (or ignore) the possibility that the work is simply not as good as an older, less
"innovative" book or film.

The Establishment perpetuates itself through the maintenance of unfair, biased "hierarchies" that imply the inequality of participants.

Status emerges from human relationships because men are
basically unequal. They possess different talents, abilities,
and capabilities. Some men are able to assume many responsibilities; others are unable to meet even the slightest professional obligations. In any society, the emergence of leaders
and followers is predictable, and in no way a basic deterrent
to freedom. Such distinctions should be based on ability, not
race, creed, or religion.

The new youth culture will dictate to the mass-marketing
interests, because if "the kids" only want bell-bottoms,
manufacturers will have to sell them or lose sales.

Again, this conclusion is based upon the premise that the
market is established through popular demand for products.
Most of the fads and fashions of the youth cult have been
created through advertising and public-relations campaigns.
Admittedly, some of these campaigns have been launched by
men and women who dress differently or who use different
jargon than advertising or promotional executives of ten
years ago. But despite the outward differences, these persons
have not been interested in "responding to the popular
demand"; instead, they have taken over commercial channels
of communications for the same reasons as their prede-
cessors: the sale of their products and their personal profit.
Promoters of rock groups, for example, may wear bell-
bottoms or beards, but as businessmen their attitudes are
indistinguishable from their older, less aggressive colleagues
who now seek to imitate them.

The key, therefore, to assessing the real worth of a revolution, even a non-violent revolution, is not an evaluation of
what it overthrows, but rather what it offers. Too often one
form of totalitarian regime is replaced by another totalitarian

regime. Our society, of course, is anything but totalitarian; with all its faults, which we may freely acknowledge, we should think *more* than twice before wholeheartedly replacing it with another social order. Social observers respond to the milder indiscretions and blatant immorality of some young people by talking about the "searching" generation; they emphasize general, passive activities, "searching," "knowing," "feeling," experiencing." Active, creative, dynamic, specific programs and proposals are usually ignored. The youth cult has developed no concrete individual philosophies or credos, any more than it has developed broadly based doctrines for social reform.

The youth cult, with its emphasis on dropping out is based on the assumption that individual changes will alter the entire society. Such conversion might be legitimately compared to the adoption of a religious belief by a single individual. If enough individuals subscribe to the new life-styles, we are told that these life-styles will ultimately be adopted by the majority. But we can assess the success or failure of these individual life-styles collectively. With the decline of such hippie havens as Haight-Ashbury, emphasis has been less upon dropping out of society and more upon the absorption of counterculture life-styles (music, dress, and morals) in our social mainstream. Herein lies the danger. Society will not fall apart because of a few dropouts, but it may decline through adoption of a whole variety of detrimental influences. If we examine the youth culture as a whole, what do we find?

Political dogma steeped in Marxism, little respect for individual freedom, a willingness to exploit racial differences. When forced into a concrete declaration of principles, the advocates of our "young people" offer standard, shopworn, Marxist political dogma. Even high-school students are mouthing tired old collectivist slogans. These are hardly the "new" or "exciting" answers to our social and political ills. These solutions have failed in Russia and China. The apolitical revolution is steeped in collectivism, with all its well-known evils.

The youth cult offers to replace our "culture" with its own. What is the new music, art, literature, or poetry? In the artistic fields in which the advocates of the youth cult have enjoyed free reign, what have we been offered as an alternative? A "musical art form" in which we assume profundity to be implicit in the caterwauling of anyone who plays the guitar and tries to sing? Painting which requires no special skills, or pop art which presumably tells us that our society is irrelevant. Literature or films in which a heavy emphasis upon sex and drugs is considered to be the *only* meaningful approach to any subject! An approach to the English language in which literacy is regarded as an affectation and illiteracy is glorified as an expression of the true self! In truth, the new "culture" is not the blissful product of "participants" working, as their advocates would have us believe, out of individual creative expression, rather than technical skills.

This is the "culture" of a new social order which not only glorifies dilettantism, but implies that the work of commercially exploited illiterates or amateurs is superior to the work of anyone who is skilled. In the musical profession, even the most distinguished composers have been forced out of work to make room for unskilled persons who play the guitar or sing with no special talents or abilities. The new "culture" is supposed to be noncompetitive; in reality, it is a competitor. Writers of non-sensational novels or screenplays are already encountering difficulties similar to those which hastened the professional demise of many fine composers. If their works do not conform to the youth-oriented syndrome developed by an open-minded, "non-competitive" élite, these writers can forget their careers too. In the new youth culture, the brillant artist and the impudent ignoramus are equal; if the former does not express his "equality" by imitating the latter, he is eliminated.

The new youth cult replaces refinement and dignity with crudity, casualness, and impudence. In the new youth cult, presumably dominated by "affection" or mutual respect," social graces are regarded as "affectations", so are all forms of courtesy or refinement. Youthful arrogance does not allow for the fact that all of the *progress* as well as the negative elements in our society was achieved by former generations.

The youth cult replaces cleanliness with filth. Charles Reich speaks glowingly of the day when the President of the United States "will have to don bell-bottoms and a dirty shirt" and go searching for his constituents. Advocates of the new "culture" are not in the least disturbed by the implication that activities exist in the realm of human endeavor which require reverence, dignity, personal cleanliness, or serious and respectful demeanor. According to the new "culture" man can play the same "role" everywhere, all of the time. But man is not fulfilling the same functions twenty-four hours a day.

The youth cult replaces order with disorder. Its adherents often like to assume that "order" implies repression because it provides an easy and accessible excuse to applaud disorder. Rock groups have been offered as an example of the ideal, communal way of life. The feuds, lawsuits, and petty disagreements that have permeated the professional associations of these groups are a matter of public record. Promoters of such gatherings are quick to publicize them as "celebrations of life," implying that middle America and conservative parents should be eager to apologize for misunderstanding their intentions. Yet these "celebrations" are a prime example of the youth cult's ineptitude.

In Puerto Rico, thirty thousand youngsters attended a rock festival. The result? Three hundred hippies at the airport without funds and unable to return home. The festival included three drownings, a murder, and a considerable number of lesser crimes. A Miami newsman said he was nearly knocked off his feet by "the stench of marijuana." These young people advertise their complete inability to participate in an orderly society every time they attend such a gathering. In Puerto Rico, the civil defense organization had to be called in for help.

Legitimate status distinctions are replaced by new, artificial distinctions, based not on merit or achievement, but on "implied equality." Status distinctions are supposed to represent the dependence of society upon artifice and formality. This dependence serves to perpetuate the Establishment. We are told that doctors behave as if they are "superior" to nurses, bosses behave as if they have the right to "boss" their employees, teachers have authority over their students, etc. Ostensibly to dignify the working man, we are advised to forget about the authority of one individual over another.

This neat ideological bubble is quick to burst. The only alternative to a society that preserves status distinctions is a society run by an endless number of committees, composed presumably of persons who have been stamped, sealed, and certified "equals." A major university in mainland China is run on this basis, with the top administrators responsible to a non-college graduate, a people's representative. (We can imagine the outcry if the faculty of Harvard were made responsible to a "hardhat.") In truth, we cannot obliterate differences in ability or leadership potential by pretending that the formal trappings of authority have been abandoned. A good teacher must take charge of his class, regardless of whether he tries to be friendly with students. If this non-status approach were carried to its logical extreme, surgeons would allow interns and nurses to express an equal diagnostic voice in the operating room. Pilots, who exercise obvious control over whether the plane goes up or down, east or west, would suffer a similar fate. Passengers and stewardesses would be able to operate the controls. In school, kindergarden students could vote to decide whether or not they want to read, write, or spell, and devote themselves to the less strenuous activities of life. Ultimately the folly of artistic incompetents and ignoramuses could be extended to all forms of human endeavor. In government, important decisions could be made by thousands of additional committees instead of individuals. Umpires would be eliminated from sports, with decisions made "equally" by fans, depending on who screams loudest.

The use of the uneducated to oversee the activities of professors would be an effective way of seeing that they did not veer far from state-approved "people's policies." Those who seek to abolish all forms of authority are really trying to transfer authority to themselves. The society controlled by "people's committees" is really controlled not by the people but by the bureaucrats, functioning under orders from those who successfully control the bureaucracy. Cries of "black power" or "student power" often emanate from those who seek power not for blacks or students, but for themselves as the self-appointed spokesmen for a group. Society must have leaders and followers. Inequities do exist, and these should be corrected, but not by pretending to abolish "status," so that employees or students can declare themselves "leaders" of groups which never elected them, as an excuse to exploit society for their own gain.

The youth cult reverses leadership roles between the generations. Parents are expected to devote their time to purging themselves of a collective sense of "guilt." They regard their children as guileless and virtuous, and consider the "progressive" life-style of their offspring to be sacrosanct. Parents thus become followers, seeking to emulate their children in order to relieve their sense of "guilt" regarding the ills of the world. The younger generation assumes the lead; the question is not whether the children can grow up to follow the ideals of their parents, but whether the parents can somehow obtain the "approval" of the younger generation by admitting their guilt and eliminating it by subscribing to the tenets of the youth cult.

Naturally the parents are encouraged to regard ideas which conflict with the new culture as old-fashioned and irrelevant, by definition. If the youth cult is founded upon cultural illiteracy, abstention from personal cleanliness, drug addiction, or amoral social values, these elements are granted a new respectability because they are identified with youth. The idea of parents following the spiritual beneficence of their "innocent" children might be valid if members of the younger generation were either "innocent" or "children." But this standard does not apply to adherents of the youth cult. A pair of middle-aged parents whose greatest aim in life is to identify with youth through adoption of long hair, long sideburns, mini-skirts, bell-bottoms, teenage jargon, dependence on drugs, and a futile search for the fountain of youth are making fools of themselves. Parents should be concerned about setting good examples for their children, not assuming that "what the kids want" is necessarily right and proper just because children are chronologically closer to achieving the state of youth. Fathers and mothers should be interested in being leaders, not imitators. They have better things to do with their time than constantly wondering if they have managed to go "where it's at." The fact that a man of fifty succeeds in growing sideburns which were popularly grown to that length during the days of Chester A. Arthur or William McKinley does not mean that he is "young" or that his ideas about raising children are necessarily correct.

The youth cult proposes to replace "the system" with a "systemless society." Unfortunately, society cannot survive without systems. If all governments were abolished, private individuals would invariably try to seize power. The youth movement reputedly encourages men to "roll in the grass and lie in the sun." No one explains who is going to pay for these individuals' well-being. Unless they begin receiving welfare checks out of other men's pockets, their source of income becomes a matter of public concern. If they can support themselves, their life-style is their own business, to the degree that their behavior does not infringe upon the rights of others. But persons do not live in a vacuum. If they choose to wander around without visible means of support, they cannot be permitted to become public nuisances. Some suggest that individuals selecting their vocations should not be intimidated by whether such a choice represents an established occupation, defined and accepted by society. This is all very well and good in theory; but in practice, careers which are not "established occupations" may well infringe upon the general welfare of other citizens. A man has a perfect right to consider himself a poet if he so chooses; but if his pursuit of *la vie bohéme* means that he may expect hard-working citizens to support him, or to pay for his food and clothing by stealing, his life-style is treading upon the rights of others.

The youth cult fosters an adjustable moral standard, in reality a double standard used to exonerate its adherents or justify the very acts on their part that they condemn in others. One cannot divorce the youth movement from its political agitators or the chaotic violence of rock festivals. We cannot pretend that the new "culture" is divorced from its more unpleasant advocates. Society cannot pretend that Jerry Rubin's obscenities are "meaningful" simply because he chooses to wrap himself in a cloak of idealistic respectability. Advocates of the youth cult are quick to condemn "violence" or "immorality" among police officers, businessmen, or hardhat construction workers. They are careful never to do so when referring to campus mobs or drug peddlers.

The implication that the "revolution of the now generation" is divorced from violence and immorality is hollow indeed. In truth, the new youth movements represent a headlong flight from responsibility. "Morality" does not signify doing whatever is pleasant or fashionable at the moment. Until the youth cult repudiates its dependence on drugs, obscenity, filth, squalor, and violence, we can only regard its "revolutionary" potential as equivalent to the outcry of spoiled children. These are not children, however, but young adults, fully capable of dismantling our society and replacing it with one of their own.

The youth cult ignores the forgotten Americans. Thousands of persons of all ages want the "good life." They want peace, freedom, and opportunity to find the best mode of living for themselves and their families. Foremost among the forgotten Americans are the young people who do not adhere to the tenets of the youth movement. A college student who does not choose to follow his "leaders" on campus may be subject to social or political ostracism by students or faculty who may possess influence. The young executive who does not give the impression that he is a "bright, young man," fully communicative with "the kids" and "what they want" may be started on the road to professional failure. The parent who tries to maintain discipline, respect, or an intelligent perspective regarding the "old" values may be subjected to the full retaliation of the permissive society.

The youth cult venerates an élite group of "heroes" who
become the favored few and models for emulation. Although
the youth cult ostensibly deplores status seekers, it encourages the mass adulation of false idols who often possess no
redeeming qualities whatsoever. Leaders of rock groups,
anarchists, and even Communists become nationally known
celebrities who enjoy fame, publicity, lucrative lecture fees,
television and radio coverage, and popularity. Although these
"heroes" often dress in old clothes or feign identification
with the "common man," they function as stars, often
enjoying a life-style which is as ostentatious as that of film
stars of yesteryear.

The most curious aspect of the youth cult is that it
adopts the very standard young people are supposed to find
ridiculous and immoral in the values of The Establishment.
By assuming that money and material success are their own
justification, they rationalize the blatant immorality of those
young people who achieve it.

The Continental Hyatt House, a hotel located on the
Sunset Strip in Los Angeles, near over thirty record companies, decided to take advantage of its location. It has become
what Time Magazine called "a psychedelic pantheon for
anybody seeking a Woodstock ambience with a bacchanalian
bounce." In short, the hotel encourages rock stars to patro-
nize it regularly. The result is hardly an example of idealistic
decorum.

Young people can easily observe (or read about) the
behavior of their favorite stars. Members of the Led Zeppelin
broke their own record for damage at the hotel, $2500
worth, surpassing the $1700 worth of damage they did in
1972. They destroyed paintings, soiled walls, submerged ste-
reos in bathtubs, tossed ice cubes out of the windows at
passing police cruisers, and dunked mink-clad women in the
swimming pool. The J. Geils Band staged mustard and ket-
chup orgies in their room. Joe Cocker stomped his birthday
cake into the carpet. The Electric Light Orchestra gave a
party, and a groupie had so overindulged in narcotics that
she was propped up in the corner of an elevator. She rode

up and down for an hour and a half before anyone discovered she was there.

Teenagers, for all their claims to maturity, are impressionable. If Alice Cooper's groupies and roadies (young people who follow the group from place to place, hoping to have contact with their idols) can play nude football in the hotel hallway, what is to deter Billy and Susie down the block? If teenage idols can stage motorcycle races in the hall or deposit LSD in the coffee cream, they are rewarded by becoming rich and famous. Very little attention has been paid to the groups who follow rock stars as part of their traveling aggregation. The Hyatt House reported that transvestite crowds following Alice Cooper and David Bowie have included persons dressed as a ladybug or the Tin Man from "The Wizard of Oz".

In effect, we are told that people's behavior is justified because they pay for the damage. Destruction of private property is rationalized because the perpetrators of these acts have enough money to indulge their whims. The youth cult is presumably furious at the thought of adult hypocrisy, but young people are encouraged to emulate their idols in every sense of the word by competing to see who can be the least responsible in personal lifestyles.

Although we are constantly told that each generation of children grows into a progressively more sophisticated generation of teenagers, we tend to forget that young people can be as impressionable and as conformist-oriented as a flock of sheep. Consider the frustrated teenagers down the block who resent the millions of dollars earned by their equally untalented counterparts on television. Consider the justifiably frustrated young men and women at college who cannot find a forum for their views because they are too responsible to merit the attention of those who publicize and promote only the sensational. Such emulation can only court distorted values.

Those who talk incessantly about the Establishment fail to credit the youth culture with its greatest success. Although many young people oppose the cult, American

society today is engaged in its own destruction by a pernicious effort to subject every social and cultural component
to the standards and capricious whims of the new youth
movement. It is a revolution steeped in irresponsibility,
vulgarity, and childish temperament. Is is a revolution that
seeks not a renaissance of ideals, but a new social order
under the cloak of idealism. It is a revolution which demands conformity to all its mores and folkways. It is a
revolution to which many "mature" Americans seem eager
to capitulate. It is a revolution which easily identifies what it
is against, but not what it advocates. It is a revolution that
glorifies the primitive and debases the civilized. It is a revolution that functions in a moral vacuum. It is a revolution that
seeks to destroy our society, debunk our culture, and de-
grade our values. It is a revolution that seeks to accomplish
these things by accusing non-believers of the cardinal sin: the
crime of maturity. It is a young revolution, an evil revolution, and though some of its adherents possess the best
intentions, we must remember all too well where the road of
good intentions can lead.

X.

BLUEPRINT FOR PROGRESS:
A POSITIVE ANSWER TO THE YOUTH CULT

The true reformer will not only hate evil, but will earnestly endeavor
to fill its place with good . . . . Charles Simmons

"A family without government," says Matthew Henry, "is like a
house without a roof, exposed to every wind that blows." He might
better have said: "like a house in flames, a sense of confusion, and
commonly too hot to live in." . . . . Henri Frederic Amiel

If we cannot find the answers to today's problems in the
creation of a youth cult, we must discover solutions somewhere else. It is easy enough to recognize the weaknesses in
theories advanced by radicals or to laugh at the foolishness
of middle-aged adolescents who applaud them. This is the
first step; the second and most important step, however,
may be achieved by the substitution of a legitimate interpretation of these same events. There is no panacea, no
instant solution. But positive alternatives do exist; it is our
duty to discover them and our responsibility to see that they
are not obscured by simplistic rationalization or childish
tantrums.

The greatest danger presented by the youth cult becomes
apparent when we realize that a number of its suppositions
in regard to society are true. Men are often preoccupied with
materialistic goals; they are often immoral and hypocritical.

Our priorities have often become confused; our life-styles have not brought us instant happiness. Unfortunately, as has been demonstrated in previous pages, the youth cult itself is actually a negative, highly deleterious result of our confusion. The youth cult is founded on the assumption that any number of elements identified with social progress go together. This is false. Often mature adults are drawn to the youth cult in spite of the fact that the new "culture" stands for all the qualities they may abhor. We may discern a blueprint for progress by calling upon our common sense and mature intelligence to recognize our current social difficulties for what they are.

In every instance in which a society which depended on the "old values" has created difficulties for itself, it has actually ignored the "old values" while pretending to uphold them. Thus, we see quickly that our institutions are not at fault, but rather, our human tendencies to do these institutions a disservice. Therefore, let us seek to achieve the following:

. . . **Distinguish between** change and progress. Ideas are not "good" because they are "new" or "bad" because they are "old." War, poverty, immorality and disease are as "old" as time. They are as "new" as yesterday's newspaper.

. . . **Recognize that** time-honored principles and traditions are often time honored because they work. We must constantly recall an important corollary of this principle: a return to "old" values does not necessarily imply retrogression.

. . . **Be certain** that if institutions are to be abolished or replaced, they will be succeeded by other institutions of greater value to society.

Advocates of the new culture insist that the status (or survival) of our political and economic institutions is irrelevant and insignificant until individual life-styles change.

It has become intellectually fashionable to leap before you look. We court disaster if we discard institutions, without the foggiest notion of how these elements will be replaced. Our positive response is to re-examine these institutions and to improve them. If marriages have often ended in divorce or unhappiness, the youth cult adherents say, "Marriage is out. Eliminate marriage." This is clearly a flight from responsibility. If marriages have not worked over long periods of time, it is because men and women have not made them work. If families are not close, middle-aged adolescents are quick to declare that "It's because parents don't understand what the kids want."

They beg the question. Family relationships do not work well because something is wrong, and that something is far more complex than the satisfaction of youthful idealism. One positive step is the assumption of responsibility by members of the family unit. Fathers and mothers would do well to consider the confusion that results when both parents are busily pursuing full time careers. Parents should start setting examples for the children, not the other way around.

Lawrence H. Fuchs, who teaches a college seminar on the American family, has insisted that the American family will re-emerge as a triumphant institution of the 1970's. He observes, "People can only hurt so long. The pain the young are feeling makes them more realistic. As they watch the wreckage around them, they seek loving and belonging. When they find no alternatives that really work, and there are none, they will think of ways to strengthen the family." We cannot sit idly by, watching our institutions fall apart; what is true regarding the family is equally true of their institutions. Only a fool would try to deny that a variety of individuals, violent and extreme, would like to see our society destroy itself. Their goal, of course, is an opportunity for them to rebuild society according to their own whims. Civilized man has come to depend upon institutions because he cannot afford to be so fatalistic as to depend upon the innate "goodness" of all other men.

We are told that, "Schools are imperfect. Tear down the schools." Nonsense! Of course, they're imperfect. Let us improve them. (In many instances, the schools can be improved by a return to some of the tested principles that made the schools successful in the first place. If colleges and universities seem to provide training which is irrelevant, educators can provide alternatives.) We are also told that, "The government is imperfect. Abolish the government." Nonsense! If we abolish the government, who will govern? No one, suggests the anarchist. Everyone will live together in one big happy society, one marvelous rock festival of love, peace, and brotherhood. But adherents of the youth cult have demonstrated time and time again that their perfect, "systemless society" of rock festivals leads us to utter chaos. The free indulgence in drugs and sex is not a discovery of this generation; ultimately, the youth cult's solution to our institutional problems is to ignore them. Instead, we are told that these problems will work themselves out after we all renounce the values of the Establishment. The rock festival is as new as the Roman orgy, and as deadly.

We are told that many of our political figures are frauds, insufferable windbags and blithering hypocrites. Like all societies, we have our share. If we want to get rid of incompetent politicians, we possess the ways and means to do so. We are told that our democracy or our republican system in a myth, that only the rich and the powerful can exert political pressure. Perhaps we need to discover new ways to influence public opinion. The civil-rights movement of the 1950's and 1960's and the public lobbyists representing conservationists are examples of constructive political action. What better means exist to eliminate incompetent political figures? In some countries, they would be exiled or shot, with similar treatment for their supporters. Some choose to tell us that, 'Idealism justifies our violence." Translated, this is equivalent to "The end justifies the means." True, Mussolini made the trains run on time, but we would be hard pressed to find excuses for his methodology.

What is the difference between constructive and destructive criticism? The former is offered in a positive spirit, with some sense of clear desire to improve or to build. The destructive critic has only vague slogans to promulgate, not specific suggestions. Indeed, the one offering destructive criticism is not interested in suggesting or proposing, but in demanding. The constructive critic says, "Let us improve our school curricula by recognizing that each student is an individual and that we need not sacrifice standards in order to make general education requirements more flexible in degree programs." The destructive critic says, "All power to the people! My group demands power to change the schools to suit us! " It is not very difficult to distinguish between the two varieties.

... **Encourage action** based upon positive goals, not a sense of collective guilt. Many well-meaning individuals render themselves incapable of exercising a positive influence even to the smallest degree. That nugatory middle-aged adolescents are so eager to please, so willing to prove their desire to purge themselves of guilt, so ready to be "open-minded," that they render themselves ideologically impotent.

We are confronted by a situation that is unparalleled in American history. Today, if certain "young intellectuals," were to suggest to certain middle-aged citizens that they could cleanse themselves of their "guilt" by jumping into the lake, the response would be predictable: the middle-aged morons would be quick to reply: "Thanks, kids. Which lake should we jump into? "

... **Acknowledge that** alternative life-styles exist as prac-ticed by non-conformist young people. We refer, of course, to the real non-conformists, those who refuse to join the conformist youth cult. Middle-aged apologists are often eager to dichotomize, to divide society into a neat bipartite divi-sion: old fogies and progressives; bigoted conservatives cling-ing to antedeluvian glories and kindly, beneficent professors who wear long hair and understand "what the kids want." This simplistic approach to sociology is convenient because it divides society into a handy group of heroes and villains who may be easily identified by speech, manner, and dress. Fortunately, such divisions do not hold up under close scrutiny.

Many young Americans do not espouse the radical, irre-sponsible politics or bizarre behavior which are popularly associated with the younger generation. It is unfortunate that these young people must constantly defend themselves as "squares" or "conformists." In a society that bends itself over backward to publicize its radicals, the conservative

becomes the true non-conformist for he fails to run with the
pack. The primitive world of the dropouts of the 1960's was
portrayed as the future society, an image of progress. The
true non-conformists recognize that the counterculture had
nothing to offer in the first place, so there is little reason for
society to emulate it. The hippie sub-culture represented
chaos; now we are advised to emulate that sub-culture in
mainstream society, ignoring its primitive, retarded nature.
The dropouts conformed to a society which rejected all
meaningful values. Those young people who held onto their
values during these turbulent times are the real future leaders
of America. They deserve to be recognized as such, not
dismissed as members of the Establishment who are too
unsophisticated to recognize the worth of psychedelic anarchy as Paradise Lost.

    . . . **Re-examine our** sense of values. One does not have to
be young to recognize dishonesty or hypocrisy in business. If
we cheat on our taxes, we are being dishonest. If we cheat
or lie in business dealings, we are being hypocritical. The
great error of the counterculture was the assumption that its
own prejudicial dogma is an automatically required alternative to these unethical forms of behavior. The drug culture
has no relationship with honesty in business. Neither does
the glorification of slobbism.

    The dropout society was riddled with violence and
misery. Many young people are beginning to realize that
dropping out of society is not the answer, and that our
nation can improve through constructive, positive action. But
laudatory goals cannot be achieved if we welcome to the
mainstream of society in the 1970's those elements of the
dropout culture who could not survive the 1960's. We need
more than a muddled apology for the drug mystique, the
brutal anarchists of the New Left, the artificially prepackaged pop culture which debunks excellence, the obscenity,
irresponsibility, and filth which permeates the youth cult.

    Kenneth Kenniston, Professor of Psychology at Yale, has
stated that "culture has been so far too much of a counterculture, too much defined by opposition to the evils which
you correctly perceived in American society, too much an

outcry against our culture's failure to fulfill its promises or to build upon its achievements. The student movement, for understandable reasons, has so far largely been a movement of opposition." Kenniston went on to counsel a new alliance between the Americans of all ages, between youthful idealism and the "hard work, persistence, and dedication that has characterized the old culture."

This of course, will be well and good if the alliance is achieved through a mutual recognition by the generations of the human qualities found in both categories. Too often, some young people have assumed their own moral purity while treating those who did not agree with them as moral lepers. This attitude can only succeed in provoking a response of hostility, especially when the youth culture is decidedly vulnerable on a variety of charges ranging from impraticality to immorality.

In the last decade, our society has been shaken by adults who are so eager to acknowledge their own mistakes, that they overlook the inconsistencies and errors of those who criticize them. Young adults may find it difficult to trust those members of the older generation who preach morality and practice hypocrisy. But the remainder of the society in which we live should not have to pay their price by accepting the destructive, critical view of those who issue their non-negotiable demands, but who are immature to the extent of being unable to demonstrate a single shred of personal or social responsibility. If we recognize such Achilles' heels in the youthful armor of the revolutionaries, we will protect society in the long run.

True idealism does not blend with the youth cult. We can try to understand why many middle-aged adults are eager to link them in an ideal relationship. We don't like to think of the "kids" as they are: vulgar, crude, presumptuous, and spoiled. Their idealism does not justify such uncouth behavior. We are eager to follow the lead of columnist Ann Landers who says, "A generation that is against the Vietnam War, outspoken in behalf of equal opportunities for minority groups, dedicated to fighting pollution and saving our environment can't be all bad."

All bad. Precisely the point. Some of the unwashed drop-outs may indeed have an interest in nature or in peaceful living. This does not deny that, despite their positive qualities, they negate the latter with their faults, which may be overpowering. The Ann Landers comment came in response to a concerned parent who had visited colleges, trying to evaluate them for a seventeen-year-old daughter. The parent described the "students" in their "dirty unisex clothing, unshaven, mop-haired males, braless girls in shawls, jeans, sandals and faded hiphuggers." Also obvious were lack of manners, dependence on obscenity, and the usual signs that the youth cult was thriving.

We want to tell ourselves that the "idealism" of "the kids" is really what matters. We want to forget that the youth cult is essentially a manifestation of parents' failure. Not the failure urged by those who seek to establish collective guilt! Not the failure to "understand" the kids! Instead, it is the product of the parents' (and teachers and government officials') decision to abrogate their responsibilities.

The classic example of a parent displaying more than a little eagerness to "understand" the morality gap was Betty Ford's observation regarding her daughter's private life. Mrs. Ford said that she would "understand" if her daughter Susan chose to enjoy a premarital relationship. Members of the news media were quick to issue enthusiastic support. "Why," they demanded, "should we not expect the President's family to be different than the typical American family, influenced by trends, styles, and fashions in morality? " The point, of course, is that leadership is achieved by setting one's sights above the lowest common denominator in society, not by lowering one's own standards in order to seem *au courant* with the masses.

As part of the American Bicentennial celebrations many citizens began to study the political and social issues which related to the early days of colonial government in the United States. Much less attention was paid to the question of morality in the historical development of our civilization. In particular, we seemed to forget that moral goals are achieved by striving for perfection, for absolute standards, even though these standards must invariably be adjusted to human frailty. By trying to be better than we are, even better than we can, we succeed. By following the lead of the least ethical in society, we simply insure our own decline.

Why must one become a slob to understand idealism? What does drug addiction have to do with morality? Why do we pretend to see a relationship between the lessening of materialistic pressures (i.e., keeping up with the Joneses, trying to become the world's wealthiest man) and the exaltation of mediocrity (i.e., rock music, obscene poetry, illiterate literature, and "art" forms which require as a prerequisite total artistic incompetence)?

If the youth cult said, "Enjoy your work, or else find some work you can enjoy," and stopped there, we could not object. Too many citizens become caught up in the drive for power, the drive for wealth, and a mechanized routine of daily living. Pursuing one's own special talents or abilities is a fine idea. A redefinition of "success" is in order. We may well define success as the achievement of one's personal excellence in accordance with one's individual capabilities. If a man is a good father, or a woman is a good mother, they are "successful," according to this standard.

Examples of this redefinition are numerous. The classroom teacher becomes more concerned with teaching and working with his students than with achieving status distinctions on campus as a committee chairman. A businessman may find that his hobbies may be of an artistic nature. Perhaps his devotion to painting or writing or to studying nature may take time away from his work. If he spends his weekends with his family, instead of devoting that time to his office, his career may "suffer," but his life may be more meaningful.

Unfortunately, the youth cult doesn't stop there. It doesn't even begin there. Instead, it offers us the "new values" wrapped up in a package of slobbism. Redefinition of one's values is not only highly desirable, but often essential in today's technological society. But when a non-materialistic sense of values is linked with these other elements, which may be found at the very heart of the youth cult, the idealism becomes poisoned and perverted. We are offered not the joys of idyllic Utopia, but the primitive chaos of the Woodstock subculture.

The alternative is to respond to the voices of radicalism with reason.

... **Make decisions** based upon your own conscience, not the collective guilt or conformity of others. Bertrand Russell, hardly a conservative, once remarked, "If fifty million people say a foolish thing, it is still a foolish thing." Peer-group pressure still proves itself capable of stampeding the public into behaving foolishly; people are always afraid of being different. A nation of sheep is a nation waiting for a hungry wolf. A young drug addict testified, "Kids today won't listen to parents, teachers, police, or anybody except their peers. Peer-group pressure is the only thing that is going to take the kids off drugs." The old truism, "If you can't beat them, join them" can prove disastrous in these present times of trial.

If you're going to take action, have a good reason, not just the excuse that everyone else is doing the same thing.

Frank S. Hogan, a leading Democrat and District Attorney of New York City for over thirty years, advised, "One of the saddest things in my experience is a definite decline in morality, to say nothing of the sins against life and property. The licentiousness, the filthiness of the motion picture, the underground press, so called, the theater — things that are accepted now." He went on to remind us, "Thus more and more young people say, 'It's the "in" thing. Nothing wrong with it. It is perfectly natural.' The same argument is made about drugs, especially marijuana."

Supreme Court Justice, Lewis F. Powell, levelled criticism against "doing your own thing" independent of the old-time disciplines of home, school, church, and community. He objected to an excessive tolerance of immoral conduct, and concluded, "I still believe that a sense of honor is necessary to personal self-respect, that duty, recognizing an individual subordination to community welfare, is as important as rights; that loyalty based on the trustworthiness of honorable men is still a virtue; and that work and self-discipline are as essential to individual happiness as they are to a viable society."

The views of these men are as applicable to our personal lives as they are toward our consciousness of political and social responsibility. Dr. James Anthony, director of child psychiatry at Washington University's school of medicine, has suggested that parents who are too permissive may cause painful confusion in their children.

We pride ourselves on being tolerant as human beings and as a society; this should continue. It would be a sad day for the United States if we became a nation with charity for none. But it will be an equally sad day for this nation if our zeal for tolerance renders us incapable of dealing with those political, social, and cultural challenges which can only be answered by a strong, firm hand.

. . . **Evaluate our institutions** on the basis of what they do accomplish rather than what they should accomplish. Don't conclude that an institution is obsolete because it isn't working. Our churches, for example, are suffering a variety of difficulties. A former drug addict, still a young girl, explained, "Churches aren't doing any good at all. They provide another recreation place where kids can sell drugs and get stoned." A friend of hers made similar observations about schools in which teachers permitted her to sleep when she came to school stoned on drugs. Police officers have seen a mockery made of justice, often by officers of the courts themselves. Court leniency in dealing with habitual offenders virtually has provoked a national scandal.

This does not mean that we should do away with our schools and churches, abolish our courts, or turn society inside-out. We should not assume that institutions are working, simply because they are there; neither should we abolish those traditions or practices that are essential to a civilized society, simply because they have been mismanaged or allowed to decline in capability. District Attorney Cecil Hicks of Orange County (Calif.) says, "The gruesome crime just isn't shocking any more. People are exposed to it every day, in the newspapers, and particularly, on television, where it's so personal and immediate."

We must never allow a state of violence and terror to become a condition of normalcy; only by reasserting our belief in the traditional institutions that prevent violence, can we deal with these questions. Certainly, we should attend to the causes of violence as well as the aftereffects. But we must not confuse justice and mercy with bleeding demagoguery.

... **Regard high standards** of ethics and morals as a source of pride, not something of which one must be ashamed. The debunking of excellence has become popular under the egalitarian ideal; in reality, it signifies a vicious distortion of that ideal. In the United States, equality of opportunity should depend upon exertion; we cannot afford an implied levelling process undertaken by the government or by self-styled social architects to reduce our social and economic hopes and aspirations toward the lowest common denominator. William S. Gilbert declared, "When everyone is somebody then no one's anybody."

The first step in the restoration of high ideals is the elimination of mediocrity as a personal standard. We have become dependent upon labels to convince us that tired, wornout rejections of responsibility are a panacea for our national ills. Henry F. Ottinger told his English class at the University of Missouri, "Ten years ago, the people around the fountains wore saddle shoes, chinos, and long hair. Now they're barefoot, wear army fatigues and have long hair. Big revelation: it's the same bunch of people."

Progress is splendid; too often we are not offered progress, only Marxism, anarchism, collectivism, or just plain teenage rebellion packaged under a new label.

... **In making decisions** about "the views of our children," make certain that all views are considered. No generation in history has had so many self-appointed spokesmen, so many representatives whose sole claim to authority is the decibel level of their voices.

The news media, and the journalistic profession in particular, have devoted too much attention to the views of some young people and portrayed them as the views of all young men and women. It isn't necessary to look for artificially created heroes. The Jerry Rubins and Jane Fondas would be insignificant, were they not glamorized and publicized by the press. The Charles Reichs would be revealed as apologists for a youth cult that never should have existed in the first place, if the academicians would lose their fears of being considered old-fashioned. The Alice Coopers would be regarded as social curiosities if they were not treated as serious artists. The uncouth, unwashed slobs would be recognized as leaders of a massive assault upon the public taste, if they were not welcomed into the homes and salons of the liberal élite that created radical chic.

The other young people are there, trying to make their voices heard. Often they fail to do so, not because their voices are drowned out by shouts of the crowd, but because society is so concerned with placating a small minority of dissenters that it fails to heed the concerns of its most responsible members.

. . . **Revitalize the family** as an American institution. Don't be fooled by prognosticators who want to substitute the commune or some other social unit. Remember that reform, like charity, still begins at home. If we're going to improve our society, we must start by improving ourselves.

As the whole is determined by the sum of its parts, so the nation is directed by the sum of its families. Each family represents America in microcosm. One of our primary goals *must* be the re-establishment of the home as a meaningful institution in American society.

James Hamilton, a nineteenth-century English clergyman, declared, "Six things are requisite to create a "happy home."" He went on to delineate these elements. "Integrity must be the architect, and tidiness the upholsterer. It must be warmed by affection, lighted up with cheerfulness; and industry be the ventilator; renewing the atmosphere and bringing in fresh salubrity day by day; while over all as a protecting canopy and glory, nothing will suffice except the blessing of God."

These words may seem sentimental in our pseudo-sophisticated culture. But although times have changed, Hamilton's formula for a happy home still remains valid. Particularly in this period, when advocates of women's liberation are offering definitions of "home" which present a contrasting view, we must be certain of our standards.

We are told the home is a house, and that the family unit represents merely people who live in that house. Before many families achieved their present affluence, they were required by necessity to live and work together. If we reduce the concept of "family" or "home" to a series of tasks to be performed, we completely miss the true function of the home as an institution.

"Home" is not simply a place for washing, ironing, cooking, and sewing. Although these domestic activities have important roles in the home, the family must think further. Today a mother can often find substitutes for herself in washing or ironing; we need not suggest that she return to fulfill those functions by hand. But as the various household tasks continue to be delegated to machines or maids, a mother may easily assume that her maternal functions (i.e., keeping house) are being fulfilled. In turn, fathers may assume that their duties are essentially economical. As more and more mothers decide to "liberate" themselves, and join their "liberated" husbands, the family unit continues to suffer.

Families do not enjoy themselves together as they once did. Men and women are in more of a hurry today; they want to do more, faster, in less time. As they see the younger generation without any sense of direction, they would do well to remember that a man can live his life more slowly and still go further in the long run.

Today's fashionable solution to problem has been "communication." Presumably this means a dialogue between the generations. We tend to forget that a dialogue requires by definition that one party listen to another party. But "listening" does not mean that one party abandons ideals or principles in order to accomodate the other.

Too many members of the younger generation assume their own infallibility. They credit their own "youthful idealism"; they justify a flight toward folly. Too many members of the parental generation assume their own infallibility. If moral values are re-examined, young people must take the first step to maturity; they must recognize the hollow, superficial, and presumptuous aspects of the youth cult.

If some ostensibly mature parents refuse to acknowledge their own hypocrisies and inconsistencies, their errors are compounded by another group of adults. These men and women try to absolve their feelings of guilt by adopting meaningless slogans regarding "what the kids want."

Fathers and mothers must again become leaders at home! They must again put discipline, standards, and values in their proper perspective. Young men and women must eschew rebellion for its own sake and work for positive goals and constructive lives. Parents and children who lead separate lives together in the same house are not a family. Young men and women must remember that responsible reform leads to progress; irresponsible change leads only to disaster.

Family life should become a shared experience. Society should be oriented neither around the dollar nor an imaginary notion of perpetual youth. The home, for all its sentimental connotations, still represents the cornerstone of American life. Responsible men and women of all ages should join hands to reverse the trends which pervade society today. If parents and teachers had taken firm stands at the beginning, we would not be faced with a youth revolution which offers obscenity, slobbism, and drug addiction as its primary characteristics.

Such action does not imply an end to progress or an opposition to change. As we recognize the lack of a true sense of values in our society, we can begin to discover solutions. We are not in trouble because our values have been wrong, but because too many persons in both generations have displayed little concern for our values.

Many years ago, the celebrated poet, Goethe, remarked, "He is the happiest, be he king or peasant, who finds peace in his home." The passing years have not disproved his asser-

tion. If the vanishing verdant forests disturb you, plant a
tree! As the length of the work week decreases, families
should have more time to live together and to enjoy their
lives. Parents should distinguish between being martinets and
being permissive; children should learn the difference between self-expression and an egocentric sense of self-import-
ance. We cannot solve our problems by depending on to-
bacco, drugs, or psychiatrists. We cannot expect them to be
solved for us by political candidates who promise to cure
our national ills with huge financial giveaway programs.
These difficulties did not start with money; they will not
end because of it.

Instead, we must start at the bottom and work our way
back to the top; we must begin, curiously enough at the
beginning. These solutions may seem simple. A philosophical
tome may be more impressive than a family picnic; an institution may appear to be more "modern" than a long talk
between father and son or mother and daughter. Today's
young men and women are often advised to strive constantly
for independence, as if their relationships with their parents
were business relationships determined by contract. Parents
and children will have to face some hard truths about themselves. We will not solve our problems overnight. But we can
begin. By restoring the family to its rightful place in society,
we can take a first step on the long road back. We have seen
the dismal result of a society in which parental leadership is
abandoned and basic values are ignored in the name of
"change" or "progress." The home should not be a point of
departure, but a point of return. As our homes are revitalized, mature young men and women can assume the positions of leadership and responsibility denied them by the
youth cult.

. . . **Stand up and hear**! Stand up to make yourself heard:
a silent majority can stay silent for so long that when it is
ready to make itself heard, the minority refuses to let the
majority express its will. Hear what others say, but not only
hear, listen! Don't feel compelled to apologize for your
views because they seem old-fashioned or out-of-date. The
nation will continue to flounder until we stop seeking the

approval of a small, select corps of sociopolitical snobs. It is especially demanding for those with educational backgrounds to make their views known. Our society has come to mistakenly respect the verbal wizardry of the academe; a man can sound like a scholar and still think like a used-car salesman. Jargon is not insight.

In many ways, the 1960's were years of madness for our nation; our political upheavals, our social crises were often bizarre and distorted. We often attended the Mad Tea Party, with our values becoming sources of ridicule; our villains became heroes, our heroes became villains; our pride became our weakness; our weakness became our strength; our morals became our albatross, and our vices became our virtues.

But we can recover; we can rediscover those goals and values which have never really left us. They have been obscured by the skeptics, the snobs, the schemers, and the self-seekers; but they remain the cornerstone of the American tradition.

In a world that has become increasingly complex, the simple solution is often the most difficult one to find. A famous inventor once remarked that an invention best does its job if it does it simply. One of our greatest difficulties has been our attempt to complicate problems, to fear the simple. We must distinguish between that which is simple and that which is simplistic. A fear of fundamental or basic truths can pose a greater danger to our mode of reasoning than all the complexities prepared in the longest books.

In the months and years that have elapsed since the advent of the youth cult, much has happened to change our view of ourselves and our nation. We have survived wars, political scandals, and economic crises. But unlike in former times, we have emerged from these traumatic experiences with greater doubts in our own values. We tend to forget that often when our basic beliefs seem to fail us, it is not because they have left us, but because we have left them.

The youth cult has been a failure. Its bold predictions of a new world have evaporated in a time of confusion and ambiguous disillusionment. As we begin to ask ourselves why the counterculture turned into a nightmare instead of a dream, the popular psychologists claim to provide the answer. They suggest that our national spirit has undergone a "greening" or a "cleansing process"; they further insist that discussions about meaningful relationships or more personal communications are an outgrowth of the essentially humanist base of the youth culture. They do not realize that with the failure of the counterculture, we are returning to the basic needs of society: the true sense of values abandoned by the middle-aged adolescents. Instead of recognizing their own movement as an abberation, they try to regard any renaissance of our traditional values as a logical extension of their own actions. They do not realize or understand that these are the very values which the popular psychologists seek to destroy.

In contemporary American society, many of the attitudes and fads and fashions of the counterculture, have been ushered into the mainstream of our communities. We may rightfully contend that if the counterculture failed, its ideological offspring have little place in our lives. It is essential that we not only champion a return to traditional values, but that we acknowledge the fact that we need to return to these values. It is not enough to mask this return in fashionable jargon.

The sexual revolution has provided us with a society which is morally confused. One young person talked about the new rights and privileges available through "the new morality". "I'm so free, I'm lost.", he said. The lack of a conspicuous moral base is one of our principal ills. As George Gilder has written, "Before we join in the celebration, it is worth considering whether sex roles are in fact, "artificial," "rigid," and "destructive," or whether they reflect our deepest natures as men and women. One might pay some small attention to the abundant evidence that specific and exclusive sex roles, particularly the role of provider — are necessary to change destructive male adolescents into responsible citizens. When the provider role collapses, whether because of welfare or because of the earnings of the wife, the marriage tends to collapse."

Gilder goes on to wisely suggest that "Serial" and "contractual" relationships are a poor substitute for marriage, and that no marriage system has ever worked without a promise of permanence.

The concept of being so free as to be lost is not unusual today. It is the legacy of the youth cult. Gradually, we have discarded the elements which are the moral and social glue which hold an ordered and sane society together. In our zeal to embrace fads and fashions, we have simply chosen to ignore the true nature of human relationships. In our efforts to revitalize the family, we must recognize the essential contributions made by wives and mothers. They are hardly the useless drones described by the advocates of communal living. In discussing the personal relationships between men and women, we should not be fooled by the current suggestion that a physical relationship is not enough, but that these associations must be made more "meaningful" on an emotional level. This incredible circumlocution is a search for the very meaning rejected by the counterculturists of the 1960's, when they trumpeted the sexual revolution. The "free" sexual revolutionists are trying to find a word for love. They do not realize that far from being ahead of the times, they are behind by centuries.

The primary problem of values is not an exclusively American question. Recently, a television network in England banned the films of Shirley Temple from the air, because they were not "relevant" to the needs of modern children. The arbitrary assumption of what is or is not relevant strikes at the heart of the matter. Advocates of the new culture, for all their glib rhetoric, reduce human society to its lowest common denominator. Since they draw their conclusions from materialistic rather than an ethical or moral base, they assume that man's behavior can only be explained through his most primitive instincts. Yet man's spirit, his soul, if you will, is what distinguishes him from other primates. Advocates of the new "relevant" culture, assume that love, particularly romantic love, is superfluous to a discussion of the relationship between men and women. So they reduce it to a purely biological function. They assume that the relationship between parents and children may be determined only on the basis of practical function: who supports whom, who takes care of whom. The moral or personal guidance which is so important to the communication between parents and children is dismissed. The family is only regarded as an economic unit, coexisting for its own material survival.

These people fail, perhaps by ignorance, perhaps by choice, to observe the essential difference between a true family and a group of strangers living in the same place. When "The Waltons" achieved its phenomenal popularity on television, many Americans regarded the spirit of mutual caring which pervaded the television family as unique and novel. What is tragic about such assumptions is that a view of family life which was once a prototype in our nation is today a curiousity.

In the creative arts, we have little cause to wonder that the essence of the new creative spirit is ugliness. A society which sneers at man's highest emotions can only seek to glorify his lowest impulses. Music or theater often reflects the personality of the society in which it is created. Books can influence as well as mirror the attitudes of the men and women who read them.

For all the discussion about individual expression, a careful examination of the contemporary world reveals the paradox of our times. As men and women talk more and more about expressing their true selves, they mouth slogans and echo fads. We have witnessed the birth of a strange set of attitudes and ideas, fostered by a community of rigid conformists and faddists who talk about rugged individualism.

If we can become accustomed to watching live television broadcasts from the moon, we should not be surprised that we expect our solutions to earthbound problems to be exotic. Rather like falling in love with the girl next door, it *should* surprise us to learn that many of our solutions have been with us all the time.

We must abandon the rigid stereotypes of our times; we must stop talking about "the man's point of view" or "the woman's point of view", or worst of all," the viewpoint of our young people". We must recognize the basic moral truths which have been necessary to the survival of any civilizations. The word "renaissance" literally means rebirth. If we are to prevent the family from collapsing, the culture from eroding, the nation from declining, we must begin with a rebirth of all those elements which have been the cornerstone of our own civilization.

In turn, we must recognize the excesses of the 1960's for what they were. Far from rushing headlong into new movements and causes which seek to incorporate these excesses into our social structure, we must use our common sense. The assumption that only the sensational or the material is relevant is unwarranted. Man's ethical, spiritual, and cultural perspectives are not only relevant, they are essential to his survival, and ultimately to that of western civilization as well.

We are constantly in search of "new" solutions. We may be surprised to learn that the essential basis for constructive action has been with us all the time. But like the man who goes to church on Sunday and creates havoc the other six days of the week, we must renew our values and our ideals. Utopia may never exist, but we can discover new meaning in our lives by re-evaluating our sense of values together. This is the key. Values determine our goals and ideals. A society of standards, disciplines, and a moral renaissance is the only society that is really free. If we do not detour on the way, following the Pied Piper to the mythical land of Woodstock (and ensuing disaster), we may all find our way not to the youth cult, but to a mature and progressive reality.

...INSPIRATION

ALL I CAN GIVE by Richard Chaput — an inspiring story of a 34-year-old polio victim who, amazingly, blossomed into a happy civic leader and public speaker in spite of being immobilized from the neck down and of being confined to a stretcher bed.
— $.95

CHAVEZ, MAN OF THE MIGRANTS by Jean Maddern Pitrone — since 1962 Cesar Estrada Chavez has been struggling for the human rights of the impoverished Chicano migrant field laborers in the California grape fields and groves.

— $.95

UNDERSTANDING THE RECOVERING ALCOHOLIC by Kenneth Anonymous — "There are any number of volumes addressed to the problem of alcoholism, but this is the only one I know of which deals directly and in such depth from the inside with the neglected aspect of understanding the victims. I was deeply moved by the contents." *Maxwell N. Wiseman, M.D. Director of Alcoholism Control, State of Maryland.*
- $1.25

SEXUALITY, CHASTITY AND PERSONAL HANGUPS by Joseph D. Wade — Fr. Wade has more than 30 years' counselling experience and he draws on this rich source to give help with guilt feelings and scruples in the sexual area and to offer guidance and comfort to all celibates: priests, religious and lay people.

— $1.25